Graves into Gardens

A story of love, loss, hope, and laughter

Tara Claassens

Graves Into Gardens:

A story of love, loss, hope, and laughter

First Edition Published 2021

©2021 Tara Claassens.

ABN 67202641497

ISBN 9780645293104 (Paperback)

ISBN 9780645293111 (Hardcover)

W: www.gravesintogardensbook.com

E: tara@gravesintogardensbook.com

Facebook taraclaassensauthor

Instagram taraclaassensauthor

Edited by Em Hazeldean

www.emhazeldean.com

Cover & Design by Kellie Book Design

www.kelliebookdesign.com

Squishy:
And here I am, living to the fullest like you would have insisted.
Forever you occupy my heart…

The retelling of my story is just that – my version. Keep in mind my memory has been impacted by the trauma I experienced. I like to think I remember it all correctly, but other people there that day and the days that followed almost certainly had different experiences and different stories to tell – this is mine.

Author's Note

I had been thinking about the design side of this book for a little while. In a moment of divinity, I had purchased a card made by Papyrus for a loved one. On the inside was the most beautiful explanation of why their logo features a hummingbird. Hence, woven through these pages, you will find this beautiful bird and I pray you will be reminded of these words:

"Legends say that hummingbirds float free of time, carrying our hope for love, joy, and celebration. The hummingbird's delicate grace reminds us that life is rich, beauty is everywhere, every personal connection has meaning, and that laughter is life's sweetest creation."

-Papyrus

Contents

CHAPTER ONE

It left
A mark.
Every word,
Every moment,
Every sigh and
Every half smile:
It left
A mark.

d.j.

What Just Happened?

The doctor came out and walked us to another room in the Emergency Department of the hospital in Bali, Indonesia. I'm sure they do this *all* the time to tell the families what further they are doing to save their loved one's life. Said with heavy sarcasm – I do that a lot. No, if there was more they could do, they'd be back there doing it. I turned to my Mum who was behind me as we began walking down the crisp white and sterile corridor. I waved my hand in front of my neck giving her the 'no air' diving signal. I was letting her know that I knew he had died. As we all gathered in the room, his parents and brother, my Mum, sister, and brother-in-law, the doctor began speaking. In doctor speak. I have no clue what he said. I cut him off. 'Is he gone?' 'Yes,' was the reply. 'Was he in pain?' I questioned, needing some kind of silver lining. Like it would all be ok if he didn't know what was happening to him. If he didn't experience pain. 'No. It was instant.'

Just like that. Gone. Passed away. Dead. Twenty-four hours ago I was a proud bride making promises to, and receiving them, from my brand new husband; dreams filled with a future with children and a life planned out in my mind. Fast forward twenty-four hours and I was a widow. The human brain is amazing. It can sustain you and carry you through with an instinctual survival mode I pray you'll never need to use. I barely heard the shrieks from his mother. I wasn't even aware of who was in the room. I was in a state of shock. I wasn't even crying yet. Shouldn't I be crying? I wasn't comprehending that I would never see my husband again. Husband. A word I barely had the privilege of using. How was this my life? We got married yesterday. This can't be real. What just happened?

CHAPTER TWO

"And darling I will be loving
you 'til we're 70
And baby my heart could still
fall as hard at 23"

- Ed Sheeran

Once Upon A Time...

Let me tell you about my late husband Christiaan Johannes Claassens. He was South African and the eldest of three boys. As a child, he had gorgeous blue eyes and white hair. Too cute for his own good, and from what I hear – as a young boy he was cheeky. I had the privilege of crossing paths with him when he was thirty. He still had those piercing blue eyes – it was the first thing I noticed. I was twenty-five and my life had been one huge blessing. I had an amazing family (Christian mother, sport-loving father, and a brother and sister who are awesome – but I'll deny it to the end of time), great education, and I was even given the opportunity to pursue a tennis career that led me to an athletic scholarship in the United States. Well, Texas to be more specific. Texans understand the need for me to clarify, you know since Texas should be its *own* country and all. I lived in that great state for six years and got to explore most of America's unique landscape with a wonderful group of teammates who became lifelong friends. I left my college experience with two degrees, a permanently damaged right wrist, a slight twang, and the world as my oyster.

It wasn't long after I moved back to Australia that God intervened, and my life path crossed with Chris's. I worked fourty five minutes away from where my parent's house was (you know – the one I moved back into after college, *after* moving out and leaving for the US at 17! That was a fun experience to have at 23, said no one ever!). Anyway, a friend invited me to a barbecue at her place which I said I'd go to. But after finishing my supermarket job at 9pm, then driving there, and having to start my shift the next day at 6am, I didn't feel up for it. I called her to say I wouldn't come, and she didn't answer. Twice. I didn't want to be rude, so in my supermarket shirt and black pants, I knocked on her door to tell her I was exhausted and would be skipping the evening. She said to just come in for one drink, which I obliged. Before getting to the outside area I noticed a guy with piercing blue eyes. Suddenly I was super aware of my *gorgeous* outfit and lack of makeup. Horrified, I stopped my friend and raced back to the front door. I needed my black dress jacket that was in my car, and my lip gloss. Better than nothing right? That night we spoke for hours. He was a total gentleman, and funny... and did I mention his blue eyes? In the weeks and months that followed, he was out of the country a lot with his job. We got to know each other on Facebook chat. What I remember most from that time is me writing about one hundred words, and the computer telling me "Chris is typing" for about ten minutes, for it to come back with a five-word message. Funnily enough, that was pretty much our relationship. I like to talk. *A lot.* I'll never forget Chris telling people on a few occasions that bringing me to a party was the best – he just announces my arrival, sits back, opens a beer, and lets me do all the entertaining. What I loved about him was his heart, something I know that he got from his father. He treated any friend of mine as if they were his family. He had the biggest heart. He wouldn't hurt a soul, would protect those he loved fiercely, and wanted everyone to enjoy each moment. He was loyal, trustworthy, funny, and very charming (I loved his wink). He was also an adrenalin junkie – the opposite of me. He'd bungee jumped, been sky diving and had worked as a scuba diving instructor. He was constantly YouTubing videos of wingsuit flying, deep-sea diving – things that make my stomach lurch to watch. Just to paint a picture of how different we were, let me tell a little story from a trip to Singapore we took with his parents. Universal Studios had a roller coaster called The Mummy. I didn't know it was a roller coaster. I know, naïve much? On this day, Chris insisted it wasn't a roller coaster and that I should go with them. I think he thought I could be cured of my fear of roller coasters. I sat in this roller coaster-looking chair and Chris sat to my right. I immediately started crying. *Wailing.* Like a 5-year-old. I almost threw up. We hadn't even moved yet. The next five minutes were pure terrifying, stomach-lurching, fingers stabbing into Chris's arms fearful. He wrapped both arms around me and my face was buried into his shoulder the entire ride. I know this because we purchased the picture. I needed evidence of it. I was *never* doing another one. Chris unwrapped me from his arms and told me the ride was over. My eyes stayed closed and I told him he was lying. Turns out he wasn't. I was shaky, crying and Chris felt awful! In the years to come, it was a funny story we told – and he never asked me to go on another one. He was daring and adventurous and always looking for a thrill to elevate his heart rate. In our early days of getting to know each other, I was smitten. But I played it cool. I couldn't let him know. Didn't want to be the psycho girl that had already planned our lives together. The shift for him happened when I started cooking for him. With that man, the way to his heart was through his stomach. His favourite meal I'd ever made? Oh, that would be the beef wellington we saw on Master Chef that I recreated... in *seven* hours on my day off. #awesome #ihaditbad #sarcasm

Within the first couple of years, we had moved in together and Chris supported me financially as I went back to school to get a teaching degree – my ultimate dream job. I loved kids, I always have. I think my ability to communicate with children is a gift from God. Plus, mentally I'm about eleven, so it works out well. I also coached some children in tennis when I was in the US and loved every minute of it. Chris and I took some amazing vacations – Singapore, South Africa, Maldives, Bali. Not to mention weekends away on the incredible beaches of Western Australia. We were so blessed and stated it often.

My first visit to South Africa and meeting Chris's family was when I knew he was the one for me. I clicked with them all instantly and longed to be a part of it forever. His mother, Annelie, father, Chris (yes my Chris was the third Christiaan Johannes Claassens, so I refer to him as Pa Chris – easier for me!), and his two brothers, JC and Jandre. Jandre married his wife Netta on that trip, and later JC's wife Charlene would be added to the mix, as well as a few children! The Claassens clan is growing bigger and bigger, and we love it!

My love for my South African family is a bond that is so strong and an absolute blessing in my world. Anyway, back to our first visit to South Africa! It was on that trip, just before Christmas that we visited with his family in Cape Town. We went into a tanzanite store just for a "look" because it was raining and our previous plans were cancelled. I was *very* excited. Chris kept saying if we got a stone, it would be an investment. "Yes dear, of course." An investment on my second finger from the left on my left hand, sure! My favourite shape was a cushion cut. They had a small one and a large one, but not the middle one, which I wanted. Chris told me to pick. There was no way I was going to make that call. So the salesperson brought out two shots of whisky. One for each of us. Chris downed both, put the second glass down, and pointed to the large one. Whoop there it is! I couldn't stop looking at it when we got it back to his Aunt and Uncle's house. I recently visited them again and we laughed about the story of how we got it and how excited I was to show them. When we were back with his family on Christmas day, his cousin, Jackie, designed the ring with us. Looks like our "investment" was becoming a bit more. I loved a split shank ring with milgrain, to make it look timeless. Chris came up with the idea of having a 'C' and a 'T' put on either side of it. The design was amazing, I couldn't wait for it to be finished. When it finally was, and it was sent to us from South Africa, I was floored. It was better than I dreamed. A sparkling blue cushion cut tanzanite surrounded by diamonds with a split band. In the sunlight, it turned a shade of violet. I put it on, showed Chris and he loved it too. And then we put it in the safe. Where it sat. *For years.* Two, maybe three. I can't even remember. But it didn't bother me. Not at all. *Not one bit.* Ok, maybe a bit, or a lot. Ok, *maybe* I would try it on sometimes when he was away on a work trip, imagining our future and what it would be like to get engaged. Anyway, time went on and we also had a ring made for Chris. His grandfather passed away before I met him, and Chris was with him when it happened. The last thing his grandfather did was place his wedding band on Chris's finger. We had that turned into a new wedding band for Chris, with the original engraving preserved on the inside - his grandparents' initials with their wedding date. On the opposite side, we had ours inscribed. That too sat in the safe. Chris was a guy who thought and thought and overthought about everything. If there were 248078 reasons to do something and 1 not to, he'd focus on the 1. But I knew he took marriage seriously. It was a forever commitment. In conversations with his father, I realised that he instilled in Chris the seriousness of marriage; the ups and downs and how *forever* it was. So, he was terrified. I get that, and I loved him for that.

In July of 2014, we had the most magical trip to the Maldives. It turned into our dream diving trip – each day completing two varied dives - night, navigation, deep-sea, photography – whatever was available. I was filled with optimism that this was the trip where we would get engaged. The ten nights came and went and I have many wonderful memories from our time there – including dancing with Chris to a live band playing our song, *Somewhere Over The Rainbow*. Made famous by the Drew Barrymore film *Fifty First Dates*, one of our favourite movies. But alas, no engagement. On the flight home, he told me he meant to bring the ring on the trip so he could propose underwater when we were diving, but he'd forgotten. Wow, that *would* have been so romantic…

On October 20th 2014, Chris and I bought our dream car. It was a four-wheel drive that we would use to take camping trips with our children. Gone were our extravagant overseas vacations in the coming years. We were now planning for our future and our future children. As we were sitting to sign for the car Chris leaned in and said to me, 'This is a very big day for us.' I just nodded, but in my head I thought, I've signed on a car loan twice before, it's not that big of a deal.

But that was Chris, very serious by nature, thinking and overthinking everything six million times before acting, so I brushed it off. After the documents were signed we waited for the dealership to bring our car around. I looked at Chris and asked him what my third gift was going to be. The first birthday I'd had when we were dating he had given me three gifts throughout the day and told me that gifts came in threes – a tradition that continued throughout our relationship. This day, we'd got the new car, I was about to head to the mall and get a new cell phone, and I enquired as to what would be the third gift. He pulled that ring box out of his pocket and opened it. I was speechless and completely taken by surprise. *Completely*. So surprised in fact, I didn't say anything. Later, Chris told me it was the first time I'd ever had nothing to say, and that it was the worst time for it to happen. He was very nervous. I don't know why, as if there was ever a doubt. Apparently, for the second time, he asked if I'd marry him and I said, 'Oh my gosh, yes. Didn't I say that yet?' I was beside myself with excitement.

This is what it felt like. To know you were loved by someone through thick and thin for the rest of your life. To know you would be loved, supported, protected, and befriended for all of your days by this guy, always. I'd never be alone again. It felt *amazing*. I quickly called my mum and best friends and he called his family. Wow. I calmed down slightly as soon as they brought the car around. Chris took the SOLD sticker off it and placed it on my lap – I, like the car, was now his. Don't worry, I'm far too independent a woman to agree with that statement, but it was a sweet and fun gesture.

That night we popped some champagne and took a family selfie with our dog, Tungsten in front of the new car with my engagement ring on. The feeling in my heart was pure joy and contentment. The proposal to some people may not be the kind that belonged in a romance film, but to me, it was a promise from the guy I loved the most. Honestly, he could have thrown me that ring box at me whilst I was sitting on the couch in sweatpants and my answer would have been yes. I barely slept that night. I was so excited. I felt like it was Christmas morning, and I was ten years old all over again. I couldn't wait to walk into school and tell everyone I was engaged. And it was everything I hoped it would be. Working with amazing people that genuinely want the best for you is a wonderful thing, and I was so blessed to share that moment with them.

CHAPTER THREE

"Falling in love was the easy part.
Planning a wedding – yikes!"

- Neicy Nash

Let The Planning Begin

I hadn't ever dreamed of my wedding day. I'd dreamed of having a husband, being a Mrs, having a family – but not the wedding day itself. In the early stages of our engagement, it was difficult to decide whether to spend a large amount on a wedding or just go to a courthouse. I didn't think I minded either way, but I was worried one day I may regret not celebrating our love in a bigger way. We had spoken, prior to our engagement, about having a destination wedding. We love the beach, we always vacationed in beach locations and Bali was one of our favourite places. We decided together that we would do exactly that. Our friends lived all over the world. We picked an affordable location but understood that some friends and family may not be able to make it. Once we had decided where and how we'd be married, I got into it. Notice it went from *we* to I… that is a really honest way to describe the planning process. And ultimately, the year we were engaged, Chris spent about seven months of it away in Russia or Singapore for work, so it worked out perfectly that my OCD took over and got it all done. He chose the wedding invite and the food and drinks. Those major details didn't concern me – I was busy with the 38242934 minor ones! I thoroughly enjoyed every minute of it. I had the cute little planner my mum, Pauline and younger sister, Caris had bought for me with our names and engagement date on it. I had everything for our wedding day planned to absolute perfection – the wedding planner at the resort in Bali was even impressed, and I'm sure relieved.

In the months before our wedding trip, I had an Amazing Race-themed Hens Day. We were in teams and clues took us all through the Perth CBD. I never laughed so hard – but also, I was on the most competitive team. You can't switch your competitiveness on and off once you've achieved a certain level of success as an athlete. Monopoly against your little sister, shoelace tying against a six-year-old, times tables against a ten-year-old – it doesn't matter. To prove that point, I should let you know my best friend Michelle was the person who organised the event. This included ordering medals for the winning team and an additional one for me in case my team didn't win. That is why we are best friends. It allowed me to be ninety-five percent more relaxed during the day. Our team was amazing, except we had a weak link. One member was eight months pregnant and wasn't running as fast as us. We cut her loose near a hospital and gave her cab fare home – we were after a victory and she was slowing us down. It's ok, right? I promise this *is* a funny story, and the girl, Steph, even found it funny. She didn't think we'd do it and I think she's still shocked – she just underestimated our competitiveness!

CHAPTER FOUR

And I'd choose you;
In a hundred lifetimes,
In a hundred worlds,
In any version of reality,
I'd find you and
I'd choose you.

- The Chaos of Stars

I Do... But I Could Throw Up A Little

Monday, December 14th, 2015.

Our legal wedding day. We could have done it in Bali, but the cost was horrific, and it was a four hour round trip to the embassy in Denpasar. We didn't want to miss all that time we could be swimming, laying out, and frequenting the swim-up bar – no way man! We were extremely fortunate to have our best friends with us visiting from New York. Chris had known Nico and Monja for many years through work and they were two of his best friends, and they quickly became great friends of mine also. Monja was heavily pregnant with "Spot", now known by a real name. They are two fabulous people and I am so lucky they are in my life and they blessed Chris for several years. They went to the effort of building an arch in our backyard for our legal wedding! Posts adorned with cheesecloth and entwined with green vines, with buckets of fresh white lilies on each side. It was whimsical and romantic. I mean, Chris and I were content for the ceremony to take five seconds and be done, but I'm so glad they made that effort. As it turned out they couldn't be in Bali for our wedding, as Monja was at the late stage of her pregnancy. Because of this, they turned our legal ceremony into something magical and I will forever be grateful.

I got my hair done at the salon and had it all up in pins when I got home, so that it would hold its curl for the hours until our ceremony. Chris looked at me and asked, 'Is that how you're having your hair?' To which I replied, 'yes, do you like it?' 'Oh yeah, it looks great.' It was way too easy to mess with him, but to receive a compliment with a hairstyle like that shows just how sweet he was.

After I'd dressed, in my white lace dress, I went out to Nico and Monja. They both told me I looked beautiful. I'm still not good at taking compliments, but I'll never forget that moment. I told them I was so nervous I thought I was going to throw up. Nico assured me that Chris had just finished saying that same thing. Phew. For some reason that made me feel better. But I'd wanted this for so long, I didn't understand why I felt like that, I just figured everyone must. I placed a bow tie on our three-year-old Jack Russell, Tungsten, and we were all three ready to go. We only had about six people at our house that day to witness our exchange of vows. A dear friend of mine and a colleague at my school, Mark, was a celebrant so he officiated for us. Things didn't get off to a great start as Tungsten tried to have a quick taste of Mark as he entered the backyard. *Awkward.* Tungsten was put inside and he was no longer allowed as a guest at the wedding.

As legal as the service was, it didn't exactly feel real. Chris's family, my siblings and our overseas friends weren't there to hear our promises. The ceremony lasted about 10 minutes. Mark has a wicked sense of humour (probably why we get along so well) and that flowed through our service. I did a fist pump when Chris said 'I do', to which he replied, 'you got me.' Then when it was my turn, I said 'I do' and Mark chimed in with, 'that was a bit fast', followed by Chris doing a fist pump. Then came the exchanging of the rings. Oh – the rings! 'Monja – I left them in the safe.' Oops. Mark spoke encouraging, poetic words, and below is an excerpt from what he read at our ceremony.

> *The question is asked, 'is there anything more beautiful in life than a young couple clasping hands and pure hearts in the path of marriage? Can there be anything more beautiful than young love?' and the answer is given. 'Yes, there is a more beautiful thing. It is the spectacle of an old man and an old woman finishing their journey together on that path. Their hands are gnarled, but still clasped; their faces are seamed but still radiant; their hearts are physically bowed and tired, but still strong with love and devotion for one another. Yes, there is a more beautiful thing than young love. Old love.'*

To sit with your spouse at the end of sixty years together and know you'd made it. Talk about life goals. I was inspired to be the most loyal and loving wife I could be because I knew that's exactly what Chris deserved. By the end of the ceremony, my left finger had my gorgeous rings on it, gifted by my husband as a promise that he would weather life's storms with me as long we both shall live.

After going out for dinner that evening with our small number of guests, we got home and quietly watched television as we both had work the next day. I had a husband. How did my life work out so perfectly? How could one person be so blessed? God surely loved me. I was on Facebook that evening changing my name from Tara Browning to Tara Claassens. It was one of only a few posts that I can remember making in my Facebook lifetime. I was a wife. I was a Claassens. I felt privileged, loved, blissful, content, and euphoric. I didn't sleep much that night either. Who can sleep when their life is so perfect? The next day at school, one of my students had written my new name, 'Mrs Claassens' on some white paper and insisted we stuck it over top of 'Miss Browning' on my name tag. I received congratulations from my friends, colleagues, parents, and the school community. I was so joyous, grateful, filled with love and so excited for my life. I remember exactly how I felt that day, vividly.

CHAPTER FIVE

*"I came that they might have
life and have it to the full"*

John 10:10 NIV

"Off To Bali With My Husband"

That was the post I made as I checked us in on Facebook at the Perth International Airport. 'Off to Bali with my HUSBAND for our wedding.' As we sat waiting for our flight I, Tara Claassens – not Browning, had a glass of champagne and my husband had a beer, so we made a toast to how blessed we were and that we were about to embark on the best trip of our lives. Did I mention he was my *husband*? Arriving at the resort, we were taken to our suite which overlooked the ocean. It was breathtaking. Dark hardwood floors throughout, a huge king sized bed with four posts around it and lace hanging softly, a huge marbled bathroom with a massive bathtub, and a luxurious sitting area. But what took our breath away was on the far side of the room. Four doors opened to a balcony overlooking the sparkling Indian Ocean. As we stood, hand in hand, gazing out, we saw the sun shining brightly in the sky and its reflection hitting the water; a beautiful, tranquil God-gifted sight. We relaxed immediately and ordered some beverages. After all, we were all-inclusive and full luxury on this trip. Let the good times begin! We had guests arriving throughout the day and by five o'clock there was a bunch of our wedding guests on that balcony, catching up with old friends and meeting new ones. It was just as I imagined it would be. Pa Chris, Annelie, JC, Jandre, and their wives were all in Bali. For the first time in four years, the Claassens clan was united! What a special time that we treasured dearly.

Unfortunately, it was around this time we heard from my brother, Jason, that his passport had expired. He would be arriving in Bali on the 22nd of December (the day after our wedding) and still returning on his original ticket home, the next day! I asked him not to come, because it was ridiculous to go that far for such a short amount of time, but true to character he insisted.

We had two days before the wedding which were filled with so many amazing memories, fun, laughter, and love. I'm not going to lie; it was also incredibly stressful. Having people travel from all corners of the globe to see you is very difficult given the time constraints. It wasn't like our previous vacations to Bali where it was relaxation central – there was a bit of stress and edginess thrown in there. I'm sure any bride who has experienced a destination wedding would know what I'm talking about. When time is limited and you want to share it equally with everyone, it's stressful. Chris could tell. One evening, quite early, he took me to our room and said he told everyone we were having a night off. It was so thoughtful. It was just us, relaxing in the quiet and it was necessary.

CHAPTER SIX

"It's there, I know it is,
Because when I look at you,
I can feel it. And I look at you,
And I'm home."

–Finding Nemo

If You're Nervous, Don't Show Up

Monday, December 21st, 2015

It was finally here. The moment to wear my self-designed, white lace dress and have my Dad walk me down the aisle to my forever person; and make our promises to each other with our best friends and family around us. The excitement on that morning was running rampant through my veins. I know for a fact Chris was incredibly nervous – he never liked to be the centre of attention or to be on show. Honestly, as extroverted as I am, being the centre of attention wasn't my kind of thing either. I had said to him, 'if you're freaking out and super nervous, don't show up. We're already married anyway.' It was kind of a joke. I mean, I didn't want to walk up the aisle to no one, but I also didn't want him to be so anxious to the point of being sick.

We were separated early in the day. The girls need time... like *hours upon hours*, and it takes an army! I had three bridesmaids, my Mum, and myself to get hair and makeup done. The day was simply a dream. I gifted my girls with personalised glasses, robes and my bridesmaid Cathy (who also did everyone's make-up – she's one generous and talented lady!) had bought us all bags that had our caricatures on them – so sweet! We popped some champagne, listened to music, and just enjoyed the process. By about three o'clock I was getting edgy. The ceremony was scheduled for four o'clock that afternoon, but we pushed it back by thirty minutes. Just what I wanted to do to Chris, torture him for another thirty minutes, but beauty takes time. When we were done, we walked down to another room, close to where the long aisle started. Here I put on my dress, my shoes and met my Dad. Final pictures were taken and then Dad and I were out the door.

The second I stepped out, I couldn't yet see Chris or the guests (it was an *incredibly long* aisle), but I heard our song playing. *Somewhere Over the Rainbow*, the Israel

Kamakawiwi'ole version. I immediately began to cry. I had so many emotions, but the biggest was that this was the moment I'd dreamed of for a year now. It was almost overwhelming. I was so overcome with pure joy that my emotions spilled out in the form of tears. My Dad, in his manly, reassuring way encouraged me to get it together with a shoulder tap. *Awkward.* This *was* me getting it together. But that's my Dad; no-nonsense, no fuss, super caring, but in a manly way. Gotta love it. I also need to put in ink here, he is the B-Grade Port Hedland tennis champ from about 20 plus years ago (yes, he reminds me of this fact *to this day*). Google 'Port Hedland'. It's an isolated mining town in Western Australia. When I was in college we would email each other, and often the subject line from him would read B-GRADE TENNIS CHAMP. No matter how many state titles or All-Big XII First team nods I got, or even winning the number one doubles position in the conference, nothing could measure up to that achievement of his!

Back to the wedding. I could have wailed walking down that aisle, but I managed to suck it back! I did the ugliest of cries for that long walk until I could see the guests. Mum got a perfect picture of me looking horrifically distraught. It's one of my favourites. I look so terrible. Our professional photographers got one of me with tears, as I whimsically and calmly wiped it from my cheekbone... I guess that's why they're paid the big bucks. My Dad kept telling me to slow down during our walk, but I just wanted to get to Chris.

When I finally stood opposite him, he looked at me and asked if I was ok, to which I replied, 'I'm just being a sissy.' He told me I looked beautiful, the dress, my hair, my makeup. I was on a cloud, and we stood there, hand in hand, as the ceremony began. About a minute in, Chris's right hand came around and grabbed onto our clasped hands. I knew he was nervous. I too added my other hand, and there we stood, clutching each other for dear life. I knew he was nervous and that holding onto me kept him calm. I had planned the prayers that were said during our service. We would need God's help to make it through the long and winding journey of life as a married couple. Pa Chris also read a prayer he had prepared to bless our marriage. We said our vows, promising to love each other until death do us part. I can so clearly remember watching videos of our wedding in the early stages of my grief, and hearing those words was like a cruel and taunting joke. Almost as if the universe knew what was going to transpire. Sometimes my heart still struggles to hear those words at weddings, in a movie, in life. But my head is more caught up now thanks to the wonderful healing effects of time. One thing I'm certain of. We did love and cherish each other until death did part us. We walked back down the aisle that day to the song *Good Life* by One Republic. It was exactly how we felt. This life we had chosen for ourselves and that God had planned for us was going to be a good life. Team Chris and Tara were inundated with the support of the highest quality of people. Our tribe was strong, and we loved each other.

After the ceremony, we had about an hour of photographs, followed by some quiet time in the room with a few special people. Our wedding planner soon came to get us to take us to the Reception room. We were announced and made a grand entrance. It was quite mortifying, as neither of us realised that was going to happen, but we rolled with it. What followed was an evening of laughter, being silly, attempting to dance (and some *actual* dancing, because since when is the 'sprinkler' *not* dancing?), lots of mojitos, and the absolute best night we could have hoped for. We cut the wedding cake to *Thinking Out Loud* by Ed Sheeran and our first dance was another song of his, *Tenerife Sea*. It was the most magical moment. The following excerpt are my favourite lyrics from the song.

> *Should this be the last thing I see,*
> *I want you to know it's enough for me;*
> *'Cause all that you are,*
> *Is all that I'll ever need.*
> *I'm so in love.*
>
> *-Ed Sheeran*

I'm a horrible dancer, and Chris is amazing. We settled for a rock back and forth moment. I've watched the film of that first dance many, many times. We shared a kiss, we were giggling, definitely from the embarrassment of everyone watching us! Later in the evening, some traditional Afrikaans dancing featured at the feet of Chris and his family. The Proclaimers *I Would Walk 500 Miles* played on repeat until the fast pace of the dancing got the better of them. It was a great beat for their dancing. All my friends couldn't believe Chris could dance so well. I could. He had tried to teach me before Jandre's wedding and it had ended with me falling off the patio ledge. It was a fall of about 20cm, but that was enough for me to quit and get back to my classic move... the sprinkler.

By the end of the night I was *exhausted*, and even that is an understatement. Most of the guests were heading to bed, but some of our friends and family were going to kick on at the bar. I went upstairs with Chris to change before coming back down. When we walked in, it was like a dream. Rose petals were on our bed, the bath had been drawn and had a love heart in rose petals in it. We took a bath together. It took me about five minutes in that bath for the exhaustion to set in. Chris got out first and I asked him to get some clothes out for me to go back downstairs in. After a little while, he came and got me, towelled me off, and changed me into my pyjamas. I walked into the room and he'd placed a white rose on my side of the bed and had turned it down. He put me in bed and said to go to sleep. I can barely remember what he said to me, I was asleep in no time at all. I found out the next day that he'd gone back downstairs and continued to party. I suffered from FOMO that next day (fear of missing out). I hadn't wanted our magical day to end, but I couldn't keep my eyes open! It had been the most perfect day. Chris was my husband and we had a bright future ahead of us. God was so good to us.

CHAPTER SEVEN

TIME

You were the one
I wanted most
To stay.

But time could not
Be kept
At bay.

The more it goes,
The more it's gone,
The more it takes away.

– Lang Leav

Just Like Any Other Morning

I woke up the next morning to find Chris already awake (a normal occurrence for us, he never needed much sleep). We chatted about the previous day and Chris filled me in on what I'd missed when I passed out. We took in the view from our balcony and Chris waved to one of my Godsons, Maverick, who was on a balcony opposite us. We ordered some fruit from the room service menu and made a plan for the morning.

We left our room and went to spend time with my Mum and Caris in their room. We laughed, sharing memories of the wedding day – it was such a precious time that I think back on very fondly. From there, we went to his parent's room and visited with them, his two brothers and their wives. His parents presented us with a gift that blew us away. It was Chris's Grandfather's clock that he had received as an acknowledgement of his retirement. They had put a plaque on it that read 'Tara and Chris December 21st, 2015 Bali.' I knew Chris was emotional about the gift, he was always quiet and kept a lot to himself, but his eyes told me of the pride, love, and honour he felt in receiving it. The following year I regifted it to his brother and bride with an additional plaque for their wedding day. His mother had also written us a marriage poem, which Chris read to everyone. He draped his arms over my shoulders as I was seated on a chair in front of him. This was one of those moments in which I struggled to believe this was my life. I was so blessed. I don't know what I'd done to please God so much that everything in my life was so wonderful, but I sure was grateful.

From here we all went downstairs to the pool. Some stayed, others went to the beach and we continued with our vacation. Chris and my sister's husband Blake decided to go on the jet skis like they had done on two previous occasions during this trip. It took so long for the boys to get organised and go to their room and get their cash that Chris had told me he couldn't be bothered going anymore. It sounded more appealing to stay in the pool and use the swim-up bar. I had told him to just go, it wouldn't take long, and Blake wanted to. Finally, the boys were all organised and ready to go. My mum, Caris, and I were heading to the day spa with my friend JP (a nickname I gave her that stuck. Her real name is Jennifer) to use my 'wedding couple' spa voucher. Chris wasn't much into the spa scene. It wasn't manly enough for him. As we parted ways I said, 'Goodbye my husband', and gave him a quick peck, walking further on. My mum was behind me and had said, 'Goodbye my son-in-laws', to Chris and Blake. After this, Chris called her back and told her he loved her so much. Then they walked off to the beach. That was the last time I would ever talk to my husband. Less than seven days from our legal wedding. Less than twenty-four hours after our Bali wedding. It's sad. As I sit here and type it, I know it's an absolute tragedy. It's gut-wrenchingly devastating. Reading these words, you could be a stranger and just be overcome with sadness for what transpired. Because it was and is and always will be just that… sad. But the beauty of stories is they have lessons to be taught, and more stories to tell. Not a day goes by that I don't wish mine didn't have to begin with the unimaginable. I wouldn't be human if I didn't. And that's okay.

CHAPTER EIGHT

*"I could only be grateful when
I realised that I would rather
have known you for a moment
than never at all. I would rather
endure this inexplicable pain of
outliving you than to never have
seen your face, spoken your name.
I would rather be yours, and you
be mine, regardless. Regardless of
the sorrow, the sleepless nights,
and the years I will walk this
earth, carrying you in my heart."*

-Scribbles and Crumb

The Moment My Life Changed Forever

I was ten minutes into my spa experience. Mum, Caris, JP, and I were in a pool that had ridiculously strong jets in them. We were giggling, trying to control our swimsuits, and having a blast. I saw Chris' boss, a dear friend, and his best man, Deon, walking over to me. Before he got up close, I yelled to him, 'You have to try the pool out, it's incredible.' As he got closer, he replied, 'There's been an accident. You need to go to the front desk. They will tell you which hospital Chris is at.' I replied with a giggle and said, 'You're joking.' He confirmed he wasn't. Looking back, I saw his bottom lip was quivering slightly. Looking back, I know that he knew just how serious it was. In hindsight, I know he didn't want to be delivering this news to me. What an awful position to be put in that he handled with incredible grace. At that moment, I panicked, got teary, was shaking uncontrollably, and got out of the pool immediately. I went to the locker, put my sundress on, and went to the front desk with the girls. It took a little bit for the staff to understand what had happened and where I needed to go. I didn't have the full details either. I realised later that the accident had happened down the beach a little bit, not with our hotel jet ski company, but a private company a few metres further down the beach. I realised I had no cash or anything with me. JP gave me some cash and said she'd stay back and to let her know how we were going.

The hotel manager drove us to the BIMC Hospital in Nusa Dua. I was told the car ride would be ten minutes. I think it was, but it felt like hours. On the way, my sister reassured me that he'd be fine. Blake was a bull rider and rodeo clown. She had been in my exact situation many, many times. I just told her that if he was ok, I was going to kill him because *who does this on their wedding trip?* Still shaking, but knowing he probably had a broken arm or a concussion, I walked into the emergency room. That moment shook me to my core. The sterile smell engulfed my senses. I walked towards the front desk receptionists. Before I reached them, they pointed me to another section of the emergency room, easy to see as it was full walls of glass. I walked in. There was a woman, with brown eyes, and a look on her face of total compassion. When thinking about that moment, I think she wanted to be anywhere else than at work that day. She told me I needed to sit down and prepare for the worst. 'It's not good', she said. I didn't understand. I told her we'd just been married yesterday. Those big brown eyes, full of empathy and hurt for me – I was a stranger, a woman she'd never met. 'I know', she said. I've thought about that woman a lot. What was her job that day? Part of me also questions whether God sent her to me, an angel to deliver that horrendous news in the most loving, warm, empathetic, and compassionate way. A couple of years later I reached out to the hospital and found out that she was the head nurse that day and had moved to Australia. She was a huge blessing at the worst moment of my life and if I could, I'd give her a huge hug, thank her and tell her that the compassion in her eyes is imprinted on my heart forever.

Mum and Caris sat with me and we were all tearing up, anxious and unsettled. I experienced a physical sickness at that moment. I thought about throwing up, but I needed to stay calm. He could still be okay. Chris's family arrived a little bit after that. I delivered the news directly, 'It's not good at all. You need to sit down and prepare yourself for the worst.' At this news, they sat, and Chris' mum began to pray profusely. I hadn't thought to pray. I felt so much better knowing she was here, and she was praying. It could all still be okay. God couldn't let this happen, not under such cruel circumstances. I'm not sure when Blake joined us in that room. He had been in the back with Chris. He was the one that brought him there – I think??? He was nothing short of amazing during the accident and in the aftermath. I'm not sure what he experienced on the beach, in the ambulance, at the hospital, and every day since. I can only imagine it was a brutal time that no human should have to endure. But he went through it, came out to me, and was all hands on deck to do whatever we needed. Blake is an incredible human being and I am so proud to call him a member of my family.

It was then that the doctor came out and asked us to follow him. We arrived at a room and the doctor gave us the news we all feared. Chris had died. Beloved husband, son, brother, doggy daddy, and a loyal friend had now gone to heaven at the age of thirty-six, within the first week of being a husband. We also learned the details of Chris's accident. He had navigated too close to one of the moored boats on the jet ski. In Bali, the boats are moored all over the ocean, there isn't a section for mooring your boats. I assume Chris would have gone up close to a fancy one, dreaming about purchasing it one day. Who knows? The mooring line was like a thick fishing line I've been told, unable to be seen at a distance. From what I've heard, Chris went behind the boat, but only the jetski came out the other side. After being pulled from the water it was clear he had a gash on his neck from where he'd unknowingly driven right through the line. So there it was. Confirmation that the guy I love the most had died.

My person.

My best friend.

My husband.

My world.

He'd already taken his last breath. I was in shock. I remember the wailing from Annelie. I didn't know what to say or do. My experience in life so far had not prepared me for this. I don't think I fully registered everything going on around me, nor the news. It was around this time that my phone pinged with a text message. My phone wasn't on roaming and I had no access to receive or send texts. I had my phone on me in Bali primarily to use as a camera! This was the first miracle from God. My best friend, Michelle, was back at the resort and had heard there was an accident. She text me to say we can have him airlifted to a different country with better medical access. My only reply to her was to get JP to the hospital immediately. At the same time, I had also sent Blake back to the resort to get JP to be with me at the hospital.

I need to pause the story here to tell you about JP. I met her during my time in Texas. I coached her at the country club I taught at. She was my prodigy. Ok, maybe not a *prodigy*, but she was the only one that refused my instruction to run and touch the fence during a tennis lesson. 'I'll run after a ball, I am not running and touching that dang fence', she would say. Gotta love it! JP is kind, generous, remarkably empathetic, wise, hilarious and someone that everyone needs in their life (but find your own, I'm not keen to share her!). What makes her so special isn't just these amazing qualities, which in themselves are outstanding, but that she has overcome tragedy in her life when she lost her husband and eldest son many years ago. Up to that point, we had travelled to Europe, the Caribbean, and parts of the US together. She was my travel buddy and a dear friend, always quick to laugh and explore. When I heard Chris had died, I needed my Mum and Caris, but I also needed JP. She had walked this path, she had gotten that devastating news, I just needed her.

She walked into the back room of the hospital after a short time, with tears welling in her eyes and I said to her, 'I'm a widow'. I felt despair, loss, shock, and a huge amount of disbelief. She told me, 'I did not want this for you'. I'll never forget that exchange. All the laughter we had shared over the years and at that moment, I felt a bond with her that was so strong. She stayed in that room with us, she requested calming pills for me, because she assured me I'd need them. She knew what to do, at a time when we were all at a loss. I remember stating at one point, 'how much longer do I have to stay here? Can't we just leave now?' In my head, I thought I sounded callous and cold. Typical woman, I wasn't in my right mind, but could still clearly berate myself and judge my thoughts and actions at the worst moment of my life. In reality, I needed to get away from the hospital. I didn't want to be there anymore. I chose not to view his body. The thought was almost too much. I believe in these moments in life, whatever you decided to do is the right thing. There's no manual or playbook. Whatever you choose to do, is the exact right thing. In all aspects of life, we all just do our best right? Let's go easier on ourselves. For real. Starting now.

CHAPTER NINE

MOMENTS

Life changes
In moments

Each second
So different
From the next

Then
You were
A wife
Mother
Daughter
Friend

Now
You are
A widow
Griever
Mourner

The one left behind

And that one moment
Changes your world.

- Jodie McCarthy

My World Stopped But Life Goes On...

The manager of our resort was at the hospital to drive us back. As I walked out of the emergency room, two of my closest friends and colleagues, Roschel and Sarah, had arrived in a taxi, on their way to the airport to fly home. Blake had delivered the news to them. They were hysterical, as was I. We had about two minutes to hug and go our separate ways. Roschel asked me who I wanted her to tell. My reply, 'everyone, tell everyone'. At that moment, all I could think was I didn't want anyone to ask me how my wedding trip went. It was no secret I was going away in the holidays to get married, I shouted that fact from the rooftops. My greatest fear was to be asked how it went and for me to break down in tears. I needed her to let everyone in the world know. I look back at that moment, and in the early stages of grief, your brain can't process anything outside of the current minute. But once I was healthy, I realised how difficult it must have been for them to deliver that news to people. To fly home from what was supposed to be a celebration trip. Moments like these impact everyone. People you know and love, as well as strangers hearing the story. It's overwhelming how many people are impacted by a tragedy such as this. And the sad thing is, it happens every minute of every day the world over. The human spirit is incredible. We're thrown into these circumstances that seem hopeless but we're able to navigate through it stronger. Go us!

I remember staring out the window on the way back to the resort, staring at all the people bartering on the streets. I was angry. I yelled at them. How could they care about something so trivial? Who cares about saving ten dollars? The air conditioning was on in the car, but it didn't relieve the sweat trickling down my forehead. As I continued to look out the window, I remembered Chris and I standing on those streets wheeling and dealing, not just on this trip, but each of our visits to Bali. Happy holidaymakers were giggling over their fake *Gucco* and *Ray Bon* purchases. The shop keepers focused on sweeping the streets in front of their stalls with their cane brooms, the dogs wandered around, their lives all unaffected. Their life in that second was the same as it was the hour before, and the hour before that… and the one before that. Didn't they know my new husband had died? Didn't they know that every second was suffocating me? Even breathing was difficult. Don't you see me? My despair? But death happens.

Every.

Single.

Day.

A huge lesson I had to learn is that life goes on. It doesn't stop for anything. My world that day hit a stop sign. I felt like I was traveling a million miles an hour rocketing joyfully through life, to be suddenly smashed into a stop sign and I wasn't buckled in. My world stopped. I stopped. I'd hit speed bumps before where I slowed down a little but would still progress forward. But on December 22nd, 2015 at approximately one o'clock in the afternoon, my life stopped.

I got back to our hotel room and it was full speed ahead. My best friend Michelle went into work mode. Being a police officer and having worked as a member of the major crash team, she seemed to know what to do and was on the phone with the consulate immediately. To be honest, I can't tell you what she did. No idea. I know it was a lot. I just watched my best friend hit ground zero and she was a lifeline helping things progress. I may not know what she did, but I will forever be grateful. Another person I need to make mention of here is Deon. He doesn't feature much in my recollection of things because his face time with me was limited, but I know he was working overtime behind the scene. He is another person that I know handled so much on that day, and the coming days, that I was not privy to. It's incredible the people that step up and carry huge burdens without even blinking an eye. Michelle, Deon, and Blake were three such people that my gratitude will extend to for all the days of my life.

There I was back at the hotel and everything was exactly as we'd left it. It was eerily quiet and still. His wedding band was in the safe (thank goodness), his toiletries were on the sink, his clothes were in the cupboard – all untouched as if he was going to walk in and continue existing. When I retell the events of that day, I have to say, it's fuzzy. God created our brains so intricately and detailed. That we can go from the excitement of being a new bride dreaming of a future of babies and a life together in one moment, to dealing with being single at

31 the next. It's a lot to grasp. A process that takes months and I'm coming to learn, years. But I was completely numb. I think tears were falling, and I know I felt a constant sickness in my stomach, feeling frequently like I was going to throw up. I know I wasn't tired. The only certainty was that I needed to leave Bali immediately.

I began packing all our things. Our wedding clothes, our champagne toasting flutes, our wedding gifts, toiletries – the lot. At one point, Michelle told me she'd organised a funeral person in Bali named Agus, and he'd be coming to the hotel soon for me to sign some documents, including the authority to bring Chris's body home. My job now was to find a funeral home in Perth. My state of mind was frozen in shock. I sat at my laptop on the bed. I typed 'funeral home' into the Google search bar. Sometime later, Michelle asked 'Did you find one yet?' 'One what?' This conversation played out a couple more times until I managed to focus long enough to choose one. My brain then switched on to who I needed to call. My Dad still hadn't been told. When I was at the hospital, he and his wife, Rhonda, were at the airport, unable to be contacted. He had to land in Perth before he could be told. Then there was my brother, Jason. He arrived at the hotel a few hours after Chris died. Blake was waiting at the front of the resort to let him know immediately upon arrival.

I love the next part of the story. My brother had taken a bunch of rupiah out of the ATM at the airport and was ready to party big time, after all, he did only have 24 hours in Bali. He let everyone know this when he got out of the taxi stating he was ready to take Bali on and flashed all his notes. No one had a chance to interrupt him before he began that little song and dance, to let him know what happened. I love it because his world was unaffected for a little bit longer than mine. He came to Bali ready to celebrate, as he should have. He came to my hotel room, and the big brother vibe was strong that night. He was there with my other family members and friends as I signed all the documents with Agus. I cried as I asked Pa Chris if I should sign my maiden name or married name. The first time signing as Tara Claassens and it was to give Agus the authority to bring my husband's body home. I didn't know how to sign Tara Claassens yet. It was something I had thought about a lot before getting married, and it filled me with excitement. And here it was, and all I felt was deep sadness – a heart-wrenching, gut aching sadness. It's not supposed to be like this. How did it happen? And to me? So, I misspelled it, three a's instead of two. Agus also asked if we were having a burial or a cremation. Again, I looked at Pa Chris, but he said, 'You are his wife.

It's your choice, my dear'. A choice I would change my mind on a few times. I didn't know. We'd talked about how many kids we'd have, not this.

Repatriation. I pray none of you know what that word means. Flying my husband's body home – repatriation. I didn't need to know that. I had booked a seat for myself and my mum on my brother's flight the next day. I needed Chris home with me as soon as possible. I knew his family was staying through to the 26th (the date we were also going to leave). I also knew Deon and his wife, my bridesmaid Cathy, were going to stay through the 26th. My husband's vessel (how I like to refer to his body) would be in a country with his loved ones, even if it wasn't me. I didn't blink at that decision – everything in me told me to get home.

The blessing of having my brother in the room that evening is that he could share the news with my dad. We waited for his flight to land in Perth. When Jason phoned him, he had just turned his phone on and was in customs. I remember Jason saying, 'Chris is dead'. I didn't like that, saying he passed away was nicer. But it all means the same thing. I couldn't tell my dad, because I couldn't say those words. It was my turn to talk to him. He asked if I was okay. 'Not really', I said. I don't remember too much about that conversation. I remember my dad's wife Rhonda asking in the background what's wrong. I remember my dad saying 'Chris is dead'. I remember the customs officer telling him to get off his phone. I remember dad saying, 'My son in law just died, arrest me if you have to'. It was difficult for everyone to grasp. Even those that didn't know Chris but knew of our wedding. How does the groom die the next day? It's tragic. Pa Chris told me about the moment he called his sister and Chris's dear Aunt Nanna. Essentially, the woman that gave us all one final family gathering together. The first one in four years. He was calling with the heaviest of hearts to tell her of Chris' death. She was answering the phone with anticipation of happiness to hear of the wedding day. I wonder how many other friends and family members had to go through that, had to deliver that news or receive it?

I remember that first evening telling my mum I didn't want the room to be quiet. I wanted lots of people around. I was terrified of the quiet, the dark, and the loneliness. JP left that evening. She told me that leaving me was the hardest thing she ever had to do. But I knew this had to have brought up all types of emotions for her. Having her there with me the day my world changed was a blessing from God. I needed her and she was there. She now had to head home and look after herself. She left the sweetest hand-written note beside my bed. I still have it to this day. She has a heart of gold and it is an absolute privilege to have her in my world. My brother went out with Blake for an hour or so that evening and he came back with a big pink teddy from the 7-11 across the street. I cuddled it hard that night.

CHAPTER TEN

"With man this is impossible,
but not with God. All things
are possible with God."

Mark 10:2 NIV

The God Factor

I spent the early hours of the next morning texting with Monja in New York. I shared with her the final pictures I found on Chris' phone – one of the amazing sunrise from our balcony and two were of me sleeping. Not in a cute sleeping way but a deep sleep with legs and arms sprawled everywhere. Lovely. I also sent her the last picture that was ever taken of Chris and we discussed how truly happy he was. Then we text about whether he should be buried or cremated. Chris had told me once that he'd die without me, to which I responded that my house would be clean without him. *How funny am I?* I'd give anything to pick his orange work overalls up off the bathroom floor again. In those small hours, I also spent time chatting with my close friend in Adelaide, Nicole, whose husband had also passed away. When reading through the messages I can hardly believe it was me typing and being that strong. I started by stating how cruel it all was, the timing, right after our wedding, and just before Christmas. But then I wrote this:

"I've led an amazing life, I know this is a real test. But my faith will get me through."

Thanks to my Mum, I have believed in God my whole life and was christened as a child. I had been attending church regularly in Perth for about three years before Bali, but I wasn't someone that spoke openly about my faith. I guess because I didn't understand where it stood in my life. I knew I believed in God, but I didn't have a personal relationship with Him yet. Chris didn't attend church with me, but he was raised in a Christian home and was a firm believer also. I remember how pleased he was when I started going back to church with Mum, because he made a point to tell me. I told him that he could come with us too. He chose not to, but I'm sure I would have continued asking. It actually troubled me after Chris passed away – did he make it to heaven? He hadn't gone to church in so long. His path had wandered a little from Jesus. But

Monja set me straight about that. She told me that at the gates, they would have seen straight through to Chris's huge heart (because his truly was the biggest) and he would have been let right in. Perhaps that's a little too fluffy, and some Christian's would disagree, but it was exactly what I needed to hear at the time. To this day, my head and heart believe he is up there with those we've lost along the way, and I look forward to seeing him again when my time is up, hopefully after living many, many more years on this beautiful earth.

So, God wasn't the Tooth Fairy or Santa to me prior to Bali. He was real and I truly believed He was the reason my life was so wonderful. But I didn't pray to God privately, it made me incredibly uncomfortable to pray in a small group at church (and I would never pray out loud) and I thought speaking in tongues was weird and scary. I grew up in a church that was very small, in a country town, and I was the oldest in the Sunday school classes by a lot. So I spent that time colouring in Jesus or the wise men, not really learning a whole lot. The decision to be a Christian when I was older was definitely much more powerful for me than as a child who just followed what my mum did. But it really took tragedy and my world stopping to properly align the life I was living with the God I loved. Honestly, I still fall short every day. But I'm just here, trying my best and waking up to a fresh day hoping to do better. Why was my faith so steady in the moments after Chris passed? I have no clue. I've thought it over a lot. I was just at the beginning of my faith journey at this point in my life, and I believe it takes people years, sometimes a lifetime, to discover their faith and adventure with God – and it happened for me in the space of twelve months. When something awful happens and there's no explanation or reasoning behind it, you perhaps reach for the unknown. It's the only way to find a sense of peace in such deep, dark waters.

So here I was, about ten hours after Chris had passed away, professing my "faith" would get me through. To me, that's amazing. I learned something very special that night. No matter how far we may feel from God, or how long it has been since we last spoke to Him, He is always there. That's the beauty of His grace. He is simply waiting for us to initiate a conversation, and He is there.

It was also in the early hours of that morning that I wrote on my church's prayer request wall. Not a whole lot of thought went into it. I knew that I needed help. I knew that the magnitude of what I was experiencing was huge and I couldn't navigate this alone. I wrote for prayer on that wall and checked the box for a pastoral carer. I can't isolate God to one chapter in this book, He is a thread that runs through my journey. You may not be a Christian, you may be spiritual and believe in 'feelings' or 'something that is out there.' Also, you may be an atheist. You don't have to share my beliefs to read my story and journey with me. You just need to be open-minded and accept that we are all traversing the planet in the best way we can, waking up and doing our best every day. We are all different and I thank God for that. Our uniqueness is what makes the adventure of life so rewarding and inspiration filled. To tell my story honestly and faithfully is to share the amazing things God has done in and through me. So major shout out it to Him, because without His help through this journey, I don't know if I would have survived, let alone thrived.

CHAPTER ELEVEN

*The flower that blooms in
adversity is the most rare and
beautiful of all.*

- *The Emperor, Mulan*

How Beautiful Is The Water?

Late in the evening on the day of Chris's passing, our wedding planner had dropped off a USB with all our wedding pictures on it. They had told the photographer what had happened and that I was leaving the next day, so he worked on it until it was completed. At dawn the morning after Chris passed away, I went to the beach with Cathy. I took my laptop and the USB and we went over each picture. There Chris and I were in those pictures, lovingly staring into each other's eyes, hands entwined, wedding rings placed on left hands, prayers being said... I walked through my wedding day with each click of the laptop from an outside perspective. The photographers caught the emotion of the day in a series of images. I knew I was deliriously happy on that day, but I didn't notice how happy Chris was. He looked content and at peace. This made sense to me when I received an email from Mrs Park, the wife of a man Chris had worked with in Singapore, who were both our wedding guests.

Dearest Tara,

We came to your wedding with excitement, love, and aspirations. We left in sadness. Chris was blessed to have your love and care. I had bumped into him last Sunday at 10:30pm after an Italian meal in the lounge. He expressed to me he was so happy and fortunate how things turned out for him. To have met Deon and Nico, two of the best people in his life. He was married to you and that he gets to meet up with his siblings (those that he had not seen for four years) and both side's parents, all because of the wedding. Little did I know that was the last private conversation that I will ever have with him. God had a plan for him: to share with all of us his love, kindness, and his sweet smile, and genuine expressions. He will forever be in our thoughts and heart. We cannot express enough our concerns for your well-being. Please be strong and take good care of yourself. Chris is with God.

My husband never took anything for granted. He lived by the motto, 'live each day as if it was your last'. He was brought up in a Christian home and he knew God had blessed him with amazing opportunities that led to an incredible life. He knew it, didn't take it for granted, and often felt undeserving. Because that was the guy he was. His life was blessed, and he felt beyond grateful. That in itself is a lesson a lot of us can learn. We are all blessed – people focus on blessings as material things – homes, cars, vacations. None of it matters. We all die at some point. What matters is making a difference in the world while we are here. What matters is that we have clean water, food, a roof over our heads, and a handful of people that care so deeply and prioritise you so much that they are always there for you. That right there is a true measure of a successful human. My life is abundantly blessed. I enjoy travel, I have amazing friends and family, I love my job, I know I'm making a difference every day, but I never lose sight of the fact that being born in Australia is like winning the lottery. I could have easily been born in the slums of India and everyday struggle for basic human necessities like food and water. People might be impressed by our materials items, but God isn't.

Sitting on the beach, I was staring out at the water. The water that Chris had died in. But it was also the water we were married in front of. And the water was what Chris and I loved most; to dive, boat, snorkel, fish… we were beach people. The water was incredibly calm that day, slowly rolling to meet the sand. Yes, it was devastating. I struggle to find words to explain the physical pain that our emotional distress can manifest. But on that beach, at that time, twelve hours after my husband died, I felt calm. I felt that God had poured so much love into my heart. With utmost clarity, I got a clear message. It's going to be okay. If I could sit there and look out at that beach and see all the beauty and all the blessings of my life and the world around me, then it was going to be okay. I didn't hear God *speak* to me that day, I *felt* it. Experiences such as this are hard to put in words. All I can say is when I needed Him with me, in my absolute darkest moment, He was there. I was not alone, and I would be okay. The poem Footprints is a favourite of mine, and I feel my experience on the beach that day is directly related to it. A fun fact for you: I found a bookmark with Footprints printed on it a few days after Chris died, in the drawer of his side table. I took it as a sign from God and Chris. They are both there with me each step. And I was nailing it. In my ugly crying, snot riddled, no sleep, no food, barely human state, I was kicking widowhood in the butt!

FOOTPRINTS

One night I dreamed a dream.
As I was walking along the beach with my Lord.
Across the dark sky flashed scenes from my life.
For each scene, I noticed two sets of footprints in the sand,
One belonging to me and one to my Lord.
After the last scene of my life flashed before me,
I looked back at the footprints in the sand.
I noticed that at many times along the path of my life,
especially at the very lowest and saddest times,
there was only one set of footprints.
This troubled me, so I asked the Lord about it.
"Lord, you said once I decided to follow you,
You'd walk with me all the way.
But I noticed that during the saddest and most troublesome times of my life,
there was only one set of footprints.
I don't understand why, when I needed You the most, You would leave me."
He whispered, "My precious child, I love you and will never leave you
Never, ever, during your trials and testings.
When you saw only one set of footprints,
It was then that I carried you."
-Mary Stevenson

We had one last lunch that day before we flew out. All the remaining guests and family members were there. We pulled tables together on the grass in front of the restaurant at the foot of the sand. I love eating lunch like that, with a gorgeous view, outside, with people I love. I always have. This day was different because I had zero appetite and Chris wasn't there enjoying it with me. I sat on the side that faced the ocean watching people going about their business. Laying out, laughing, swimming, snorkelling. And jet skiing. Jandre asked if I wanted to swap seats so I could face the restaurant instead of watching the jet skiers whizz past. As sweet as the gesture was, it wasn't necessary. This setting was one Chris and I had enjoyed for many years together and I was determined to continue to do that. I closed my eyes and took a deep breath. As I opened them, I took notice of what was in front of me. Palm trees softly moving in the breeze, white sand meeting idyllic blue water. Picturesque serenity. I sat there observing my friends and family telling stories, laughing, and enjoying each other's company. If we can smile and laugh today, the day after Chris died – again, I felt assured that it really would all be okay. Because ultimately, even through this excruciating loss and with the bleak nothingness I felt in my heart, I still had so much to be grateful for.

CHAPTER TWELVE

THIS
Was supposed to
Should have
Was going to
Was meant to

Be different

To this

– Jodie McCarthy

My First Decision As His Wife

I'm now years into my grieving process but sharing the story of my flight home always brings a tear to my eye. I will never forget how I felt, and the longing I feel when I think about that time, to go back to that day and give myself a big hug and say, 'Chris would want you to go home. It's okay'. The two hours before the flight were fine, normal even. My brother ragging on Mum and I for making him get to the airport so early, having a drink, wasting time. Then came the moment to head to our gate. Still relatively normal. The preboarding call was made and Mum, Jason, and I were due to walk on the plane. This was somehow arranged with the airline (again, so many people did so many things for me, I don't know who gets the credit for this one). Everything became real.

And in my mind, one thing stood out as the tears flowed down my eyes and the uncontrollable noises left my mouth. My first decision as Chris's wife was to leave him in Bali. No, not leave him, abandon him. That was my thought process boarding that plane. I walked on, with flight attendants peering at me with concern, and fellow passengers staring because I couldn't contain my tears. As I type this, I just want to go back and hug that girl. Yes, she's me. But from another lifetime. And she just did her best. She made decisions based on what she thought was best at that moment.

I don't know how my legs carried me onto the plane. I'd had the thought in that instant to just stay in Bali forever. Well, at least until he was coming home. This was one time I knew I was being irrational, in retrospect. At the time, I was just distressed. Panic set in. Anxiety began. I had trouble breathing, whimpers uncontrollably escaped my mouth… *what am I doing?* That was the first time I took a Xanex. It stopped me in my tracks. I wasn't crying anymore, but I was numb. I felt like a zombie, but at least I'd stopped feeling much of anything. For that moment, it was the best option. Looking back now, I remember stepping on the plane and stepping off. I don't remember the flight. I leaned against the window, in a comatose state. When we landed, the hysterics started again. I don't remember going through immigration. At all. When we got to the bagging area a woman working for the airport took me through a separate tunnel and walked me out directly to my dad. No idea who organised that one, but I'm glad I didn't have to stand there making a scene in public with people staring. I don't blame them for the stares though, I'm sure I would have stared too. The woman asked me what had happened. I told her through my tears. I don't recall what she said next, what do you say? I've since learned through reading up on grief that in difficult times, that sometimes it's best to say nothing at all and just listen or settle in the silence. I *love* to talk, a lot. If it was an Olympic sport, I'd get the gold. But being on the receiving end of grief, I understand the importance of silence now.

The moment I saw my dad I lost it. The tears fell. He hugged me and intended on walking me directly to his car. Gotta see the humour in this situation: I was crying and numb, and he'd forgotten where he parked. Poor guy. There were a few curse words as we walked up and down a couple of parking bays. I didn't mind. How could I mind? This was not even *close* to the worst thing that can happen in life, this is just funny. When we finally found the car, Dad asked, 'Do you want a drink or a snack or something? There's an esky in the back'. I'd barely had anything to eat or drink since it all happened. No. I didn't want anything. There was a sickness-inducing pain that had taken residence in my stomach since I received word about Chris' accident. It took away any feeling of hunger, happiness… life. I realise now that Dad too was at a loss. What can he do to help his daughter? What could he possibly say or do to ease the overwhelming hurt I was experiencing? In short, there was nothing. Not a thing another human can do to help you. Be there. In silence. Just be there. To my dad, packing an esky was one way. So thoughtful. Caris and Blake picked up Mum and Jason and we all headed to my house. The house I lived in with Chris. The house that our then four-year-old dog (that we treated like a child) Tungsten was at. I'm sure he was eagerly and anxiously waiting for us to both walk through the door.

Let me hit pause here and tell you about our four-legged fur baby Tungsten. I'll never forget the day I brought him home. I picked him up and we'd been home about thirty minutes before Chris got back from work. Our routine was that Chris would walk through the front door, I'd get a kiss and he'd head to the shower. On this day, I opened the front door, he walked in straight past me and to the puppy. Times they were changing. And I couldn't compete with a six kilogram Jack Russell with a little spot on his head. Many years ago, Chris had a bad dream that Tungsten went missing, and someone brought a Jack Russell to the house insisting they found him. Chris said they wouldn't listen when he said it wasn't Tungsten because he didn't have the spot on his head! Chris taught him how to adorably beg for treats, served him T-Bone steak and scotch fillet on more than one occasion, and when I was in Singapore, sent me a picture of Tungsten that looked like he'd taken his first selfie. My two boys – two peas in a pod, and the loves of my life.

Our poor guy realised quickly something was up. Entering our home was both comforting and strange for me. It's all as I'd left it. The moment I walked through the door Tungsten was excited, jumping up, squealing, and looking for cuddles. He's a clever boy, and dogs are extremely intuitive. Besides the initial excitement of seeing me, he didn't come near me for about three weeks. I was crying, and a big mess. I figured he wanted nothing more to do with it. There were times he'd jump on the bed, look in my eyes, then leave the room. He had no time for my emotions. It's funny to think back about it, but at the time I was distraught. I was scared he knew Chris had died. What if he had a heart attack or would die of a broken heart? I couldn't handle that as well! I just needed comfort and it sure wasn't coming from my furry pal!

CHAPTER THIRTEEN

"You're off to great places!
Today is your day!
Your mountain is waiting,
So get on your way!"

– Dr. Seuss

My New Normal

That first night at home wasn't easy. I had Foxtel – thank goodness! I still wasn't sleeping. I had caught maybe four hours total since Chris has passed away. I got to watch The Heat, The Other Guys, and Tangled on repeat for about a month or more. Because let me tell you, most movies are off-limits -even Disney. Especially Disney. Plots of parents killed, children left orphaned, child slaves… the hardships endured in Disney films are never ending! Alas, they have happy endings. I sure was hopeful that my life would mirror Disney. I relied a lot on humour in my grief. Those three movies were gold. I just watched The Other Guys last night. Those movies offered an escape from my nightmare. When sleep isn't an option – watch movies. I also called the Dial a Doctor service that night. He got to my house at about 3 am. I explained my situation and asked for sleeping pills. He told me "my first advice would be for you to get a lawyer." That advice wasn't welcomed, nor was it necessary. It upset me. But I'll assume he was just doing his best. Later that evening, or maybe it was early the next morning, I did a Facebook post. I needed everyone to know what had happened. Family and close friends that needed to be told about what had transpired had been. Now I needed the universe to know. In this world of social media, it's possible to keep track of friends from high school, college, my tennis days, my parents' friends - the list is endless. Everyone shared their well wishes and sentiments about our pending nuptials in Bali. Everyone needed to learn what had happened. In addition to that, I experienced anxiety over the possibility of someone asking me how the wedding was. I experienced a lot of anxiety over the 'what ifs.' It did take me a little bit of time to realise that I just needed to conquer the mini battles that came at me one day at a time. There was enough to get anxious over and worry about without adding to that load with things that hadn't happened yet. But of course, I was asked how my wedding went on a few occasions. And it was horrible. I think it was worse for the person asking than for me. So often I found myself just smiling and telling them that it's ok, the wedding day was an absolute dream and I'm doing well, even if I wasn't. I'd lived with the reality of that day for a little while and had become used to it, but delivering that new information to someone is quite confronting for them to receive. Thanks to social media, I was able to minimalise the frequency at which it happened.

> *Facebook post 23.12.2015*
>
> *On Monday, December 14th, 2015 I legally married the man of my dreams. On December 21st we had our dream wedding with closest friends and family in Bali and it was perfect. On December 22nd, his life was taken. I'm blessed to have been his wife and will forever be a Claassens.*

That first day in Perth was filled with streams of people coming to see me. Letting me know they were praying for me, that they cared. It was lovely. At times, overwhelming and exhausting, but lovely. My world got so small in those first few days. From Europe to South Africa, to America to Asia to New Zealand. I was loved and people all over the world were grieving with me. A few times I had to put my phone away. Turn it off and put it in a drawer. Sometimes the volume of messages, calls, and comments got to be overwhelming and would cause an anxiety attack. Slowly my heart rate elevated. I couldn't catch my breath and I feel like I was drowning above water. All side effects that I was familiar with by this point. I had to lay down, in the darkness and close my eyes. Block it all out for a little bit. That was the advice I received from JP. Put that phone in a drawer and lie down. She's a wise woman.

As much as I wanted to move forward with my grieving and attack life, I couldn't. I was floating in the in-between. Chris's body wasn't home yet. I still had to decide whether to bury or cremate him. I needed to plan his funeral. I was experiencing an existence stuck in limbo. Time rolled by, but it felt as if each hour lasted for ten. I still had some huge mountains that needed climbing, the first being Christmas Day.

CHAPTER FOURTEEN

"But then I miss you,
most at Christmas time."

- Mariah Carey

There's Nothing Merry About This Christmas

Christmas Day was worse than you can imagine. We planned our wedding for December 21st so we could celebrate with family each year since Christmas is such a family-oriented gathering. Most of our family members had leave from work over that period, so it was a perfect time to gather for a wedding also. But all that planning and forethought hadn't catered to the possibility of the unimaginable. Because it was just that – unimaginable. December 25th, 2015 - I was on my third day of widowhood. Close friends and my family were with me. I was a self-labelled Mrs. Clause. I loved everything about Christmas. I played the Christmas tunes in September! I loved the corny movies. I was the first to celebrate the birth of baby Jesus. My church would put on a HUGE production. It really was the MOST wonderful time of the year. Until that year. I'm struggling to find the words to convey the emotions I experienced on that day.

We were sitting outside on my patio seating. I was crying. About Chris. About life. About everything. At one point it was about Tungsten. He still wasn't coming near me. If he dies, I won't survive it. I can't lose both of my boys. Roschel's nine-year-old son at the time was sitting with us and he told me "He's young, he's fit, he'll be right." That was that, out of the mouth of babes. My Dad gave me my Christmas gift. I can't even remember what it was now, but it was some 'man' gift for our car. My sister got cute sunglasses. I asked if I could go back to getting girl gifts again. Our dream car had been fitted with a bullbar (a wedding gift from Nico and Monja), an awning, and new tires when we were away. We were supposed to head north after we got back from Bali as a bit of a honeymoon adventure. My brother lived in Exmouth. We had planned two weeks to drive up there and head to Karijini National Park. There were tears when I went with

Mum to pick it up. I attempted to walk in, but I broke down before entering the building. I waited outside. We got engaged when we picked up that car. The emotional attachment to it was very strong. Christmas day came and went. I completely lost sight of what was important about Christmas. About the birth of Jesus. I was too caught up in my grief. I couldn't look at the absolute blessing, privilege, and huge significance of the day. It was lost on me. On that day, I had resigned myself to the fact that Christmas was now ruined for the rest of my life. Dramatic much? But what more could be expected in those early days?

CHAPTER FIFTEEN

"A million words would not bring you back. I know because I tried. Neither would a million tears, I know because I cried"

– Anonymous

He's Home

Step one was getting Chris home. Someone had told me that Bali is a third-world country, therefore it could take up to three months. I shed many tears over that. It wasn't the case though. More unnecessary causes of anxiety. He passed away December 22nd and he flew home on a flight on the evening of December 28th. I had asked the funeral director if I could go to the airport, but they didn't allow it. They said only Australian Federal Police were allowed in the area. I then asked Michelle, but the landing time in the early hours of the morning made it a ridiculous request. So I trusted the director's word when he said he would take good care of him. I'm not sure why it was so important at that moment for me to be there at the airport. I remember being extremely upset about it at the time. Looking back, for my mental health, it was probably a good thing I wasn't there. I was in my room at home and I tracked the flight. It landed at 1 am in Perth. I tracked it on my laptop from take-off to touch down. He was home. I knew his body was just his vessel. That he was already in heaven with God. I intellectually understood that. But his vessel is what I had left to cling to here on earth.

On December 29th I met with the funeral home director. The first question I asked was "Is he home?" The answer to my question blind-sighted me. "Do you want the truth?" I just repeated myself. "Is he home?" "He is here, but he's not in the best condition." I didn't need to hear that. There are many things a widow needs to hear in her grieving – that was not one of them. My friend, Mark was with me that day (the awesome guy that married us in Perth), along with my Mum and Caris. Mark shut down that conversation quickly – I was so blessed he was there on that day. Mark would also be officiating Chris's funeral. The funeral home tried to pay him, but he insisted on that money coming back to me. That is just testimony to the kind of guy Marky Mark is. Solid through and through. I decided to have Chris cremated and we would spread his ashes in Lancelin, a beach town close to Perth that we frequented for weekend getaways. In the coming days, I worked on the program, the music, the photos – all of it. By nature, I'm a Type A control freak and the blessing of all this organising and planning is that it kept my mind occupied and gave me something to do. They were things I should never have had to do. Chris and I should have been exploring our state's North. But we weren't. Because he died, and I was a thirty-one-year-old widow planning his funeral, which was scheduled for Jan 5th. But before tackling that event, I had to survive New Years'.

CHAPTER SIXTEEN

*"For last year's words belong to
last year's language and next
year's words await another voice."*

- T.S. Elliot

I Don't Want This Year To End...

New Year's Eve 2015 – a year that I never wanted to end. It was the year I married Chris. It was also the year he died. But it was a year he had existed in. He wouldn't know 2016, and I didn't want to know a year he didn't exist in. I cried myself silly that night. Like tears upon tears that would make the Iguazu Falls look like a little splash pool! Scrolling through Facebook, everyone was making resolutions, filled with excitement for the year ahead, pondering the year that was. Honestly, as great as social media can be, it can also have an adverse effect. These days I post but don't scroll. Society is consumed with the comparison trap – and I'm not participating in it. I'm not wasting time focusing on what I don't have, because what I do have is extraordinary. Add to that the fact that no one is honest on social media. Well, let me tell you, if I'm having a bad day, you will know about it. Transparency and honesty in our social media are the greatest gifts to the mental health of friends and strangers all over the world. Because we all struggle and navigate difficulties. Let's lean on each other through the hard stuff, rather than plastering fake smiles and putting forward an image of "life is perfect." I call bull crap. That New Year's Eve, I looked toward 2016 as the year I would hold a funeral service for my husband. As the year I would spread his ashes. In 2015 I got to be a wife for seven days. In 2016 I was a widow. I don't think it was denial, I knew the hours would tick by, and eventually, it would be 2016. But it didn't mean I didn't wish I had some magical button I could press and have time stand still – just for a little longer. Because honestly, 2016 terrified me. I was scared and sad and the unknown was a terrifying nemesis that I was quietly dealing with. I was a relatively confident person, but now I had become anxiety riddled, and just scared. But time ticked on. There it was. 2016. For the first time in my life, the happy was taken from New Year.

In that new year Chris's family was due to fly in from South Africa before the funeral for a ten-day trip. I immediately felt overwhelmed and stressed. Another time I put my phone away and lay down on the bed to slow my breathing. Chris and I lived in a three-bedroom, one bathroom, one toilet home. Caris and Blake were staying from Tamworth, New South Wales. Jason was visiting from Exmouth and the Claassens were traveling with six. It was a lot of bodies to try and house in my home and Mum's 3x2 villa. Friends gave mattresses and sheets and we made it work. Plus, my South African family is amazing. Their expectation for accommodations was low – they didn't expect much at all and that made the process easier. As soon as they arrived, it was a wonderful experience. To have them with me during my early stages of grief was a true blessing. We made some wonderful memories during their time here. Some tough times, but some wonderful experiences with people that I hold near to my heart. Fish and chips on Cottesloe beach, feeding Kangaroos at Caversham Park, trips to the mall, watching the sunset overlooking the city, walks in Kings Park, and many more experiences to showcase Perth. Through it, there were tears. Crying because Chris wasn't there to apply my sunscreen, crying one day as I left the house without my wedding and engagement ring, crying telling stories of Chris, crying hearing childhood stories of Chris. Crying – both tears of happiness and sadness. It was during that period I learned about joy and sadness and how they can exist in you at the same time. I was devastated and sick with sadness, yet still able to smile, although not often in the early days, smile nonetheless.

CHAPTER SEVENTEEN

*"Breathing is hard. When you
cry so much, it makes you realise
that breathing is hard."*

- David Levithan

May He Rest Peacefully

January 5th, 2016

This was the day we had a funeral service for my husband. I had requested for guests to wear bright colours. His was a life that needed to be celebrated. He would be furious to think of everyone down and sad the whole day. Life is too short for that. That was Chris. I dressed up nicely for him one last time. I went to the hair salon, which is closed on Mondays, but the owner came in and did my hair (Tyler Reid Canningvale – greatest hairdressers/psychs/people the world has ever seen!!). I did my make-up and put on a green lace dress. I looked in the mirror and told Chris it wasn't as good as the wedding day, but it's the best I could do. The funeral service was kind of like the wedding day. It's all a blur. It goes by so fast. A close friend of mine, Sue, another in the widow club, told me to film the service. It sounded weird to me. But something I'm so grateful I did because I remembered hardly any of it. I watched that video one time and then the USB it was on stopped working and it couldn't be retrieved. I think I only needed to see it once. Any more would just be a continual dagger through the heart. Because of viewing that video one time I now have limited memory of it, and that is all I need. The service was lovely and one that I know was very fitting and deserving for Chris. There were hope-filled prayers and poems read, lovely photographs shown on the slide (mainly of Chris and Tungsten, of Chris and the car, then a few of Chris and I. It's ok, I knew where I stood) and his favourite music playing. Blake read out an amazing letter written by Nico. It's something I treasure to this day. As my friend Sue had done, I wrote a letter to Chris the days after he passed away. I've included it here, as it bears my soul and gives you a great insight into our relationship. Yes, you will probably cry, but I hope you will also smile, and I pray you too will celebrate what we had.

Hi Squishy,

Well, I can't believe I'm laying here in bed, alone and you aren't here. I need to start by telling you how blessed I was to have you in my life. I loved taking care of you. It was my reason for breathing. You have changed so much in our seven years together, and even more in the most recent 12 months. I think when you proposed to me in October of last year you still didn't quite realise it meant we'd be married. The panic when I mentioned a wedding date was a bit obvious! But I'm not sure what happened in your two months in New York at the beginning of the year, but you came home and your softer side was revealed. You were so sweet. It's like it clicked that I would be your wife. I can remember many conversations with Michelle where I joked about how you weren't overly romantic, but boy did that change. The sweet texts, the little kisses, the big hugs, affectionately calling me Skutterbol (a sweet Afrikaans term that I thought was something awful!). This year you reached your potential as a partner and I had never been more in love with you. I love the text you sent me from Russia saying you were so excited to get home, get a bull bar, and head up North to Jason's. Then writing 'oh…and marrying you of course'. You were excited to be a husband, no matter how cool you tried to play it. I remember you telling me you'd do anything for me. You said "Whatever you want Tara. You can have it. I just want you and your happiness." I can honestly tell you that all I ache for is you Chris Claassens, every morning that I wake up. It's you.

We worked so well because we were the perfect complement to each other. I was super organised which you loved because you could just show up places - like on our wedding day. I talked too much and you were quiet – another thing you loved because when we went for BBQ's you said you could just announce me and sit back and enjoy your beer. You hated to travel to Europe because of the weather (even though you'd never been there!) so I enjoyed my Euro Trip with JP. In my clean house ambitions, I was constantly picking up after your messy self, even though at work you were a neat freak. Something I only just learned about you when you invited me to help you one day this year. Thirty minutes into the day you told me to "keep my station clean." I couldn't believe it! Then there was the quiet time when it was just us and our sweet Tungsten. Our senses of humour were similar, our love for Tungsten, diving, camping, and four-wheel driving. Then let's not forget the movies – the endless hours we spent in front of the TV after building a Christmas bed on the floor. It was our cherished time together that we never took for granted due to your busy work schedule.

In the days since your passing I have heard from many people about final conversations you had, final things you said. No matter whom I spoke with, it was clear you loved me, you loved your family and friends, you were loving your time in Bali and you were blissfully happy. You were the most perfect gentleman at our legal wedding ceremony in Perth (even though Tungsten couldn't be – sorry Mark), and you were even more perfect in Bali. The photos, the dancing, the cake – I know it was all for me and as I told you that night, you made all my dreams come true. The day was so magical, and I knew how much you loved me – because of your actions and your words. I'm sitting here today, so proud to be your wife.

I know I'm always the loud one with a million friends and you're the reserved, quiet one allowing few to know the real you. But dang, you have affected people all over the world. The outpouring of love for your loss is astronomical. It makes me so proud. So many people knew and loved the man you were. Deon described you as reliable and loyal in his wedding speech and my goodness you were. You were the most loyal husband, loyal friend, loyal son, loyal brother, loyal worker. Watching you care for people was a blessing in my life.

Four years ago when I travelled with you to South Africa for Jandre and Netta's wedding, I got to meet your extended family. I had never met a more amazing group of people. At that point, we'd been together three years, but it was then I knew that I wanted to be in your life forever. Your parents, your brothers, their wives – I wanted to be part of that group. We laughed so hard that we cried. It was then I saw a future with you. As a husband. As the father of my children. I never imagined that our story, which was seven years in the making, could come to such an abrupt end. Looking over our vows, and watching the video of our ceremony, "as long as you both shall live" seems like a cruel statement now. Less than 24 hours is just ridiculous. But I can say you were the PERFECT husband. Those 20 hours from when we said 'I Do' were the best of my life and you didn't put a foot wrong. How many wives can say that? I was so angry with God that next day, but I just kept looking through our wedding pictures and the pictures of you in Bali to know that you were never happier. Each day I find more and more blessings surrounding the timing of your death and I know that it was all in God's plan.

Although we didn't get to spend our 70 years together, we did a lot of living in the time we did have. Diving in Sodwana, walking with lions at Ukutula

89

Lodge, diving with Manta's in the Maldives, safari in Kruger Park, buying pearls in Broome, standing on table mountain in Cape Town, beach time in Busselton in our dream car, buying electronics in Singapore (because you loved your electronics!!!), boat time in Albany (or as you pronounced it, Alabany), roller coasters on Sentosa Island, holding hands by the pool listening to Somewhere over the Rainbow to the live band in the Maldives, pool swim-up bars in Bali, Quad biking in Lancelin and numerous four-wheel-drive trips ever since we got our dream car. And that was just what we did together. Work took you to some amazing places over the world and you had seen and done more in your thirty-six years of life than most people get to in a long lifetime.

I promise to look after Tungsten and he will now receive all the affection that I once shared between the two of you. You would be so proud of your family. They have provided constant support and have shared such sweet, kind words with me that are forever embedded in my heart. They have made me feel so loved and cherished, as they have done since the first night in Brits. Although at times I feel so alone and so far from you, I know they are there for me any time I need them.

I can't tell you how long I dreamed of being Tara Claassens – because that would just be embarrassing and awkward…because it was a LONG time. That ring sat in the safe for a while. I didn't anticipate the first time I'd sign my new name was authorising your body to be brought back home. It was a very sobering moment that was lightened when I spelled Claassens with 3 a's – I got a little carried away. Sorry xx

So please don't worry about me from heaven, I'll be calling on my friends and family and so far, I've been so wrapped in love. It has been an absolute privilege being a part of your world and you will always be in my heart. I will live each day to make you proud of me. I always knew I was blessed, and I've never taken anything in my life for granted and I will not let that awful Tuesday change this. Life is good. I'm blessed. I will proudly use your last name and never forget the person you were and the beautiful time we spent together. I will cherish you always and forever.

With all the love in my heart,

Fluffy or Mrs. Tara Claassens, with two a's, not three. xx

I called him Squishy, from Finding Nemo when Dory says "It's my squishy, and

I shall call it my squishy..." He called me Fluffy, from Despicable Me when the little girl Agnus wins a stuffed toy and says in a terrorising voice of excitement "It's so fluffy I could die." Chris would probably have had heart palpitations if he were alive to get ribbed by his mates and probably be furious with me for sharing that with the world, but hey, he's not here to defend himself. I read the above letter out loud at Chris's funeral. I was laughing through my tears. I loved him fiercely and through the time of our relationship, the purpose in my life was to make his better. That is a huge gap to leave in someone's heart. And a few years on, it's still there. It's not as big and I pray one day it will be filled again, but until that day I'm learning to take it day by day (Chris would be proud – day by day was his motto!). I found great peace in the prayers that were read at the funeral. They speak to my heart now. The comfort, solace, and love I have found in words are incredible, both reading them and writing them. I remember laying a white rose on his white casket (an ode to the rose he left on my bed on the wedding night) and the plan was to leave the room whilst guests were still in there. I didn't want to go. I couldn't take my hand off the casket. When I got the courage to take some steps, I kept looking back. I don't want to leave him. It felt so final. And I walked. Later once the room was empty, I went back in one more time and I wept. I told him goodbye but looked up to the roof. I knew he was in heaven, but this was my final goodbye with his vessel. From here he would be taken to be cremated. I kissed his casket and I walked away. As I left the funeral home an hour or so later, I asked the funeral director to take care of him and he assured me he would. From there we went on to the same pub we had our wedding dinner at on December 14th for our legal wedding. We hired out a function room and we toasted to the best guy. Stories were told, laughter reverberated through the room and we paid tribute to Chris exactly as he would have wanted. I even shared a shot of Jim Beam with my brother and sisters-in-law at the bar, Chris' drink of choice. Yes, it was disgusting, but I know it would have made Chris proud.

CHAPTER EIGHTEEN

*"Some love stories aren't epic
novels. Some are short stories,
but that doesn't make them
any less filled with love."*

– Sex and the City

My Last Night With You

January 7th, 2016

The day I got to pick up Chris's ashes. They were heavy. Much heavier than you'd presume from watching movies. They came in a navy plastic upright rectangular container. The white label had his name and other information on it. And I carried it like it was precious cargo, evidence of the fact I wasn't coping. It sat on my bed stand that last night whilst I continued the rotation of watching those three movies. Sometimes I picked it up. I also had the thought of tucking it into bed beside me. Let's all just agree that we're glad I don't act upon that last thought (yikes). Although, in those moments, whatever you "choose" to do is ok. Considering I wasn't eating, sleeping, or functioning as a normal human if I wanted to chat with that container all night and pour it a cup of tea – well that was just fine and dandy.

CHAPTER NINETEEN

*"How lucky am I to
have something that makes
saying goodbye hard."*

- Winnie the Pooh

Back To The Water

January 8th we ventured on our road trip to Lancelin to spread the ashes. A one-night-only stay to do the ashes and show Chris's family the place we had spent many weekends – camping, quad biking, four-wheel driving, snorkelling, swimming, and making incredible memories. Honestly, I don't remember much from the drive at all. I remember the house we stayed in, but mainly I remember the need to get his ashes spread and have it be done. I think I just wanted to get it over with. In my mind, it was the last step of all the goodbyes before I would wake up and begin my 'life' again. A new life. One that wasn't my choice but that I'd been lumped with. I was anxious, sick to my stomach, sad and I just wanted it done. I remember we kept driving to find the perfect bit of beach where it wasn't windy, but I just didn't care. Let's just do it. A spot was chosen. My Mum, Blake, Caris, Netta, and two of Chris's workmates, Dave and Chris, stayed on the beach as myself and Chris's family walked out to a knee-level depth of water. I was the first and last person to scatter the ashes. It was sad. Awful. Horrible. But I also want to say, if it had been a comedy, they would have focused on how the container seemed to be never-ending. There were just so many ashes! If I watched that comedy, similar to the Big Lebowski when the ashes were windswept back into their face, I would have laughed. But this was no movie. This was reality. This was MY reality. And there were tears and hugs in abundance. Honestly, the second we were walking back to the beach, I felt a weight lifted. It was finally done. As we began walking up the sand, someone pointed out a dolphin. So close to the shore…and by itself. I knew dolphins travelled in pods. We all got excited. Mum screamed "Chris," (no, we don't believe in reincarnation, we are Christians. But could Chris or God, or the two of them together have sent this lone dolphin to tell us 'Thanks, everyone. I'll be watching you all. Don't worry about me. Gods got me. You live your best life. I love you.') Jandre was back in the water so fast to catch up to it, with his wife Netta on the beach screaming at him in Afrikaans because she thought it was a shark he was running to. Funny, lots of laughter in amongst the tears. Those two emotions – again co-existing. In the shallows, you can find joy. I'll never forget the first time I laughed after Chris died. Caris and I were laying on my bed scrolling through Facebook. It became evident our Mum had confused the crying emoji with the laughing with tears emoji. For example, our Mum posted "beautiful service for my son-in-law, Chris. You will be missed. [laughing with tears emoji]." Yes, we are awful daughters. No, we didn't tell her as we were fearful we'd upset her more. Our friend did. It's hard to be ok with laughing when your husband lives in heaven. Especially those initial weeks. I was told I'd lost the sparkle in my eye. That upset me. I'd always been the loud, outgoing, positive, and fun one. Probably annoyingly so. About a week after that a workmate and friend told me they thought I was always happy because I'd never gone through anything bad. But she said that even after losing Chris, I still had the same positive, happy disposition and that it was something ingrained in who I was. Interesting thought there, we can choose the attitude we have through it all. I could have chosen to be bitter, sullen, quiet, angry, and sad for the rest of my life. But what would that have meant for the quality of my life? Chris had died, not me. Now more than ever I realise how precious every single day is. I need to make it all count, for Chris as much as for myself. Eventually, I returned to my joyous self. It took a while. Experiencing tragedy as I did knocks you. For a little while, you believe it is the end of you. But you slowly pick yourself up, you slowly put one foot in front of the other, and you slowly start to live again. Because what is my other option? To die? For what? No thank you. Life is a precious gift, and seasons happen. My season of grief absolutely kicked my butt. But I grew from it. Instead of it being the thing that destroyed me, it became the thing that ignited me.

CHAPTER TWENTY

"Life's under no obligation to give us what we expect"

- Margaret Mitchell

Decisions, Decisions, Decisions

I was contacted by the Jet Ski company almost immediately upon my return to Australia. It was clear they were worried about being sued. I was emailed the documentation Chris had signed that waivered any liability in case of accident or death, but they stated there was a company life insurance in case of death. Looking over Chris's signature, I noticed he hadn't signed, and the initials weren't in his handwriting. It actually looked like Caris'. I took a picture with my phone and sent it to her. She told me she had signed his initials in the hospital. A man came to her and she thought he was from the hospital. I was infuriated. The priority of the jet ski staff was to cover their own butts and follow us to the hospital to get a signature they should have got before Chris using the jetski. They weren't concerned for his wellbeing or checking on the family. My grief was wild in the initial weeks and my anger was thrown into this scenario with full force. I remember one day after school, finding a tree on the school oval and sitting under it with Roschel. That afternoon I had to decide how I would handle the situation. I'd spoken to my brother on the phone a week earlier and he thought I was ridiculous for considering suing. "Why?" he had asked me. "If you sue, the company will close down and the local workers will lose their job. The jet ski company is Russian-owned, and their insurers will cover paying you the amount you sue for. Two things will happen, the locals will lose their job and be unable to provide for their families anymore and you will get money." I love people. I love the Indonesian people. My heart couldn't deal if I was the reason people went hungry. "But what if I sued and they changed the laws about the mooring of the boats so I could prevent this happening to someone else?" I asked my brother. "Indonesia is third world. The laws won't change." I remember being angry with him after that phone call. But sitting under that tree that day it was all clear. So I wrote an email from my phone, under that tree, explaining that the way their staff conducted themselves after the accident wasn't good enough. Although I understood they were worried they didn't get his signature, following us to the hospital was the absolute incorrect thing to do. I decided I wasn't going to sue, but I didn't tell them that in my email. Looking back, that was just my way of being a little bit of a brat. I just left them to worry about it for the coming twelve months (or whatever period you have to decide to sue). I'm not proud of that at all. But in grief, we do things that are based on raw emotion and hurt as opposed to thought-out intellect. I was vindictive and thought I wanted someone to pay. Lucky Jason was wise and thoughtful enough to think of the big picture. What I had to accept, was that Chris was gone. And he wasn't coming back.

I wish that was the only decision I had to make during that period. But alas, it wasn't even close. Should I bury him or cremate him? Do we spread the ashes here and in South Africa, or do I keep the ashes? Bank appointments day after day, lawyer appointments, changing all the bills into my name, meaning having to explain he had died over and over and over again. Because Chris didn't have a will, it also meant waiting for Letters of Administration before I could do ANYTHING. There was also a lot of financial STUFF to be dealt with, and all I want to say is that I navigated this with my South African family – and they are the most incredible people. It was a difficult time when Chris passed, two incomes down to one, but the same amount of bills. I refused help. But with all the legal stuff with finances, the character of every member of his family stood true. I could not ask for more gracious, kind and awesome people to be related to!

CHAPTER TWENTY ONE

*"Strength doesn't come from
winning. Your struggles develop
your strength. When you go
through hardships and decide not
to surrender. That is strength."*

- Mahatma Gandhi

Perspective and Perseverance

Let me paint a clear picture of my grief journey. I experienced an horrific event. One that I will carry with me until I take my last breath. Not just the emotions of missing Chris, but the suffering and psychological effects (PTSD – Post Traumatic Stress Disorder and memory loss) of experiencing the trauma of Bali. I want you to understand that every single day, whether spent in tears, laughing, adventuring, being terrified – whatever. Not one day has been wasted. Every day I've been growing into a stronger human being. I was listening to a podcast by Hank Fortener recently, and in it, he interviews a singer named Silah. She had to overcome so much adversity in her life. Something she said resonated with me so profoundly. "What if our problems aren't a problem? What if what happened is my greatest asset? What if what happened means I was chosen? Special? What if those things in my mind I think are holding me back actually mean I'm destined for greatness?" Talk about perspective shifting. I was blown away. I was encouraged. I was awakened. I needed to use this event, this huge tragedy. I can't waste it. That quote runs parallel to a quote from one of my favourite books by William P. Young, *The Shack*. Below is an excerpt from the book.

> *"Just because I work incredible good out of unspeakable tragedies doesn't mean I orchestrate the tragedies. Don't ever assume that my using something means I caused it or that I needed it to accomplish my purposes. That will only lead you to false notions about me. Grace doesn't depend on suffering to exist, but where there is suffering you will find grace in many facets and colours."*
> *- God to Mack, the lead character whose daughter was murdered.*

God's grace combined with a positive attitude, for me, made my worst days survivable. And so far, I've conquered all of my worst days. It's an unwavering, almost stubborn will, to get up every single day and just keep showing up. Over time, it gets easier. It never goes away. People that expect you to just "get over it" and "move on" have either never experienced grief, or they encountered it, but shoved it so far down that they never addressed it. One way is healthy, and one way means you will forever be back at the starting point, never making gains, never living a full, wonderful life. Grief must be navigated THROUGH. And it sucks. Some days I would get into bed at 3 pm. The pain was too strong. I'd fought it all day and I was in a world of hurt. If I fell asleep, I could wake up and God willing, I would wake up to a fresh start with the sadness having left my body and it would be a better day. For the most part – it was. Early on, there were three occasions when day after day the pain was too great. The longest was seven days in a row. But again, I survived it. Minute by minute. I had to be disciplined. I prayed, I was prayed for and I continued to show up. One foot in front of the other. Above all else, being a Christian enabled me to face my crisis with vigorous confidence. The red sea was parted, Goliath was overcome, the storms were calmed, the blind could see – my circumstance could be overcome. I was in a small group situation at my church recently and a lovely woman that was passionate about God encouraged everyone that was walking through hardships to just "lean into God. He is powerful enough to handle it for you. Give Him your fears and pain." Whilst I agree with everything she said, I also need to stress, as I did to her, that it's difficult. I think it's important for Christians particularly to understand that, although intellectually I understand everything she said, the heart is sometimes slower to follow amid a storm. I felt the love of Jesus poured into my heart, but I didn't physically feel a hug, I didn't walk into a home that was filled with noise and people. I was alone. And my home was empty. And I was a widow. And I love God. And He is faithful, and He always will be. But being a Christian is difficult. If it wasn't, everyone would do it. If I'm honest, it's difficult to take advice on grief and leaning on God from someone that hasn't walked the path. The divide between your intellect and your heart is huge in the early stages of grief. I was at Kids Club at church and we were chatting about a bible story in which a guy named Daniel was told he would be killed if he couldn't interpret the King's dream. We were discussing this awful time for Daniel and one of the girls raised her hand and said "it's important to have bad times in your life so that you get to see just how real God is. If you don't have anything wrong, how can God prove he loves you?" What an incredible statement to be made at ten years old. She understood. It's easy to say you're Christian if you haven't had to weather a storm or two. It's in these battles we must remain steadfast in God and trust Him to bring us through the storm, stronger and having grown. We need to strengthen our faith and our belief that in His timing it will all be revealed.

I remember being in the first term of school for 2016 and I became ill with a virus. That was what I would call the beginning of a huge downward spiral for me. I'd taken a week off work. When my body broke down physically, my mental health followed. I wasn't showering, I wasn't getting out of bed at all, I'd become a vessel. I began existing, not living. I isolated myself. Offers from friends to pop in were ignored. I was close to rock bottom. I knew I just needed to get up and shower. I'd existed in isolation for seven days. And the hurt was pulsating through me. I wish no one that level of sadness. Stubbornly and angrily on the night of day seven, I ventured out of bed. I was a mess of tears and out loud sobbing as I undressed and got into the shower. As I stood in the shower, head bowed, shoulders slumped, angry tears erupted. I was so angry with God. I yelled out loud to Him. "You said you'd walk this with me! You made me feel like it would all be ok! And here I am, alone and not coping! I feel like I'm drowning here and you left me. Where are you???" I got out of the shower, put fresh clothes on, and got back into bed. That night, I managed to get a full and peaceful night's sleep, something that had alluded me for the six nights prior. When I awoke the next morning, the sadness that had occupied most of the space in my stomach had disappeared. I felt lighter. I didn't feel sad. That experience for me was an integral part of my faith journey. Not only did God accept my anger towards Him and answer my prayers, but I also realised that in the six days before that night I hadn't spoken to God. He had never abandoned me, He was just politely waiting in the background to be called on. I was still new in my faith and hadn't fully developed a one-on-one relationship with Him yet, so prayer wasn't instinctual. I had to remember to do it. Well, didn't I feel like a jerk! Giving our creator a mighty talking too, when in fact I had only needed to call for His help. But God and I have a lovely relationship. We have great banter – he's a funny guy and I think he likes my sarcasm also…but don't be fooled – I'm terrified of Him. Like any child should be of their Father. So yes, pray. If you haven't before, start small, at home. It'll be weird. Particularly if you're not even sure if He's real. I can assure you however, He has followed you your entire life, just waiting for you to invite Him into it. Courageously step into that space. Welcome Him, give Him a shout-out. What have you got to lose? Do it! You can go from dreaming of the life you want to LIVING the life HE wrote for you. You'll find a prayer for first-timers at the back of this book. Just read it out loud. Happy praying.

"This is the confidence we have in approaching God: that if we ask anything according to his will, he hears us."
1 John 5:14 NIV

I understand the importance now of prayer and giving praise in the good times and seeking His help in the bad. And that lesson was learned through a good old-fashioned dummy spit in the shower.

CHAPTER TWENTY TWO

*"A bird sitting on a tree is never
afraid of the branch breaking
because its trust is not on the
branch but on its own wings.
Always believe in yourself."*

– unknown

Attitude

It was around this time I realised I needed a major shift in my mentality. So many of us need this. A serious attitude adjustment. Yes, you, like I, have probably been dealt a super crappy hand. Cry about it. Loud and hard. Get it out. Then dry your eyes and shift your perspective (maybe even read chapter twenty-one again).

"For a star to be born there is one thing that must happen: a gaseous nebula must collapse. So collapse. Crumble. Fall apart. This is not your destruction. This is your birth." – Zoe Skylar

We are given one chance at life. We don't know when it will end, but we know it will. Make it glorious. Make it fabulous. Make it brilliant. Make sure you LOVE IT. Don't waste a single one of your difficult days. Make it count. The trials and tribulations are the makings of us. Lean into it. That's what I work hard to do every single day. Living is a gift. A gift that many people don't get the privilege to do. So make it count! Some people choose a path of destruction which is why they end up with a bad attitude. Some people don't choose their circumstances and through this 'bad luck' develop a trace of bitterness and a bad attitude. Whatever the reason, your character will shine through. How you react to these adversities is one hundred percent in your control. It's a choice we make. Do we choose to LIVE or do we choose to stumble through life? Do we choose to shine through the storm or do we choose to sit down and get poured on? Take back the control. Live YOUR life on YOUR terms. That's how I looked at it. There are times when I think, why me? Why us? I wish it didn't happen. But unfortunately, that does nothing. I sit with those emotions for a little bit. I want to process all of the emotions I feel. I want to validate them. Of course I would feel this way. But I'm not going to stay there. Onwards and upwards. Big and bright. Bold and brave. At times, small and scared...nevertheless, one foot in front of the other, forward momentum with a smile.

I remember standing at the foot of the Christ the Redeemer statue in Brazil, in absolute awe. I could see the wounds on the hands of this statue. It was overwhelming. A visual reminder of what was sacrificed for me. A woman who sins, who isn't deserving, who, although I try tirelessly, always falls short. How incredible is God's grace? I read something recently on Proverbs 31 Facebook page that brought me back to that moment. It was speaking into scars and how we shouldn't hide them. "It's in the process where wounds turn to scars, victory happens, we regain our life in Christ and God is glorified." Amen to that. That was exactly my experience. With time, solitude, healing, and GOD, the good stuff happened. When people think of Tara Claassens, I want them to think of a brave, independent, honest, resilient, loving, and kind person who, with God's help, turned tragedy into triumph and she didn't let it destroy her, she used it to fuel the fire of an epic existence. All because I orchestrated a shift in my attitude and I chose positive over negative. How will you react to your adversities? How will you strengthen your character? Not your reputation – not what people think about you, but who you are when no one is watching. Be proud of that person. Work every single day to build your character into a masterpiece. It's so worth it.

CHAPTER TWENTY THREE

Surround yourself with people who
love your light…and add to it!

– Karen Salmansohn

Surrounded By Those Who Loved Him The Most

After we spread Chris's ashes, his family went back to South Africa and I humbly accepted an invitation and plane ticket to visit Nico, Monja, Deon, Cathy, and their son, Kyle, in New York. I felt a little bit isolated in my grief in Perth. Chris didn't know too many people outside of my family and workmates, so I felt a longing to be with those who loved him as much as I did. So our family in New York (Long Island to be more specific) was exactly where my heart told me to be. I still had three weeks left of my six-week summer break from school, and what better place to heal than in the company of our best friends and those people that loved him as much as I did. So off I adventured with a broken heart, fragile emotions, and in search of healing. My time was spent making lovely warm meals, building snowmen, making snow angels, drinking hot coffee looking out at the snow, and just cherishing the peace and tranquillity that their warm home offered me. It was on this trip that I noticed I was finding joy and pleasure in things that I would usually take for granted. As I looked out at the vast water, that would eventually join the Atlantic Ocean, buttoned up like the Michelin Man, I took steps on what was once white sand and on that day was soft, white snow. It led up to the water's edge. I'd never seen anything like it. Beaches are abundant in Australia, but to see the white sand layered in the snow was a unique image that I treasure. The heated floorboards were another new experience for me. To have on fluffy socks and feel the warmth radiate through to your toes and beyond. It was so comforting and something I'm sure people take for granted every single day. It was like I was more aware. My senses were on high alert. Intellectually I was seeking joy and finding it in the mundane. Eventually, my time in the United States was coming to an end. I had to get back as the new school year was beginning at the end of the month. I also had to start getting into the paperwork side of having a spouse pass away. That is detailed, traumatic, and never-ending. So best to get it done. Monja passed me a note that I read on the plane. She was seven months pregnant and just had her dear friend visit in the initial journey of her grief. How she dealt with those emotions I'll never know. But she's tough. Below is an excerpt from that letter. She is a quality person I'm proud to call my friend.

Letter from Monja:

> "*This time spent with you has been so special to us. It was wonderful to laugh with you and reflect on past adventures with you and Chris and to remember the anecdotes that made Chris so uniquely Chris…You are an incredible individual with the most beautiful heart and I know that you are strong enough to get through this tough time because you have decided to focus on the good and kind things that happen every day. We will keep you in our hearts and prayers…*"

CHAPTER TWENTY FOUR

"Gratitude is a description of a successful mode of living. The thankful heart opens our eyes to a multitude of blessings that continually surround us."

- James E. Faust

Gratitude

A big life lesson through my journey was a focus on gratitude. Being thankful for what I do have, not crying over what I don't have. Wake up thankful. Every single morning. Write it down. Make a list. Society today makes such a big deal out of what we don't have, focus on what you do. If you're going to focus on what someone doesn't have, let it be a child living in the poverty of a third world country through no fault of their own. First worlders, we are beyond blessed. We have so much to be thankful for. We want for too much. Our dream car, then our next dream car. Same with the house, the holidays. It's never enough. Be grateful for what you do have today and make it a priority to focus on that. It will do the world of good for your soul. Since I'm on a roll with this spiel, I'm also going to encourage you to play your small part in this big world of ours and make a difference. I went to a church conference recently and the song "I Was Here" by Beyonce, was sung. Beyonce performed it at the United Nations World Humanitarian Day in 2012. The YouTube video gave me goosebumps.

I want to leave my footprints on the sand of time
Know there was something that, something that I left behind
When I leave this world, I'll leave no regrets
Leave something to remember, so they won't forget
I was here, I lived, I loved, I was here
I did, I've done, everything that I wanted
And it was more than I thought it would be
I will leave my mark, soul, everyone will know, I was here

So get out there – volunteer, donate, sponsor a child, go on mission trips – I promise, it's an amazing way to navigate your hardships and you'll be helping the world! Get inspired!!! But honestly, if you need further inspiration, Ann

Voskamp's *One Thousand Gifts* is incredible. I mean, over a million people have read it! The way she can string a sentence together is a true gift from God. It's a brilliant read and she encourages a joy-filled existence in the mundane every day of life.

"I know there is poor and hideous suffering, and I've seen the hungry and the guns that go to war. I have lived pain, and my life can tell: I only deepen the wound of the world when I neglect to give thanks for the early light dappled through leaves and the heavy perfume of wild roses in early July and the song of crickets on humid nights and the rivers that run and the stars that rise and the rain that falls and all the good things that a good God gives. Why would the world need more anger, more outrage? How does it save the world to reject unabashed joy when it is joy that saves us? Rejecting joy to stand in solidarity with the suffering doesn't rescue the suffering. The converse does. The brave who focus on all things good and all things beautiful and all things true, even in the small, who give thanks for it and discover joy even in the here and now, they are the change agents who bring fullest light to all the world."

– Ann Voskamp, One Thousand Gifts

According to the Merriam-Webster dictionary, gratitude is the state of being thankful; readiness to show appreciation for and to return kindness. Imagine how truly content we would all be if we could live our day-to-day from a place of gratitude.

CHAPTER TWENTY FIVE

Slightly battered, deeply bruised, and tired of the strained days. Certainly, she had the right to give up, or give in, to toss out whatever fight she had left within. But she refused. She knew it a fool's fate to quit after she's made it this far. And she instead, felt compelled to pick herself back up. Brush the dust off her spirits, and with the slightest of smiles, decided that this place, right here, this space is the perfect place to start this story from. The story of who she would become.

- J. Raymond

Mental Health

How can I document my journey and NOT talk about mental health? We invest so much money in our physical health, but we lose focus of our mental health. I began seeing a psychologist and a pastoral carer within the initial weeks of Chris passing away. I'll never forget sitting in the waiting room of the psych's office that first day. My sister had driven me and was in a coffee shop waiting for me. I went to the counter and gave my name and said I had an appointment. They gave me a few pages of paperwork that first-time clients fill out. Name, date of birth, address, phone number...marital status. There it was. Single, married, defacto, separated, divorced, widowed. I never got to tick the married box. I moved straight from single to widowed. My palms got sweaty and I internally was trying to remain calm. My heart raced and my eyes were beginning to fill with tears. They began rolling down my face and I just continued to fill out the paperwork. "How happy were you this week," on a scale of 1-10. "Did you feel you had no purpose this week," "Did you want to harm yourself this week." It went on and on. By the time I was done I was silent, but tears were flooding my face and neck. As I took the form back to the receptionist I said in my quietest whisper (because that is all my voice box could produce) "do you know how much longer until I'll be in?" She looked instantly concerned. I remember feeling embarrassed. The waiting room was filled with people waiting for their appointments. She said it would probably be ten more minutes. Fantastic. There's that sarcasm again. "It's just, it's the first time I ticked widow." "Sorry," she replied awkwardly. I survived that, and every other thing in-between I guess. But that was not a fun experience AT ALL. I went through four psychs until I found my person. One left, one spent an hour telling me about himself then I paid $180... excellent. But honestly, finding the right psych, counsellor or pastoral carer is vital. It's like choosing a life partner. I mean, for it to be fruitful, you need to bear your soul to this person! Since I found a psych I click with, the experience has been eye-opening, challenging, and a great investment in who I am as a person. I'm blessed that teachers get six free sessions from the Department of Education. I value that so much. If you own a business, invest in the mental health of your people, because unfortunately in Australia, psych sessions are expensive, and most health insurances don't value it. Such a crime to humanity – no sarcasm there! I think I also fell into a terrifying category of people that shine and smile even though there is darkness festering inside of them. The poem below puts it perfectly into words. We must be asking those we care for if they're ok. And mean it. And not accepting a brush-off or a one-word answer. Because quite often, they aren't ok.

SUFFERING IN SILENCE
It is absolutely terrifying
The kind of deep suffering
The happiest looking people
Are able to hide inside themselves.
-Nikita Gill

Whilst I'm advocating hard for mental health, let me bring up the subject of medication, from my personal opinion and perspective, keeping in mind I'm not a doctor. Yes, I believe there are chemical imbalances in the brain of some human beings that can only be corrected with medication. These people, when they aren't on medication, feel overwhelmingly sad, whether they have a reason to be or not. Hallelujah for these medications! Then there are other people, such as myself, who experience horrific tragedies. I can't stress this enough. When you experience a tragedy, you are going to feel sad. For an extended period. You don't necessarily have depression; you could just be having a completely normal reaction to a serious life event. When you take pills (like I did on my flight home), it pushes your feelings down so you don't experience them. But I promise you, the second you stop taking the pills, your sadness is there, right where you left it. Make sure you deal with your emotions as they arrive. We are a society that medicates far too quickly. I was asked by a psychologist early on if I thought I needed to be on anti-depressants. My reply was, should I not be sad right now? Should I not be crying? Should I not be struggling to see a way through the pain? Are these not the usual reactions I'm experiencing? She agreed that for that what had happened, my reactions were appropriate. Then no, I don't need medication for it. There is a fine line. Be true to yourself and your journey. Your gut is good at guiding you through these situations. Trust it and go with it.

To add to the theme of mental health, something that goes hand in hand with it – exercise. I know…this isn't the bit where I'm like, go run five miles and life will be sorted. WRONG. It's also not exercising to become a size six or to look better in your clothes or whatever other crappy thoughts society has placed in your head. I'm saying 'exercise' because it's VITAL for your mental health. After landing from New York, the summer break had finished in Australia and I was back to teaching and life was resuming, my routine was re-established. I loved to run. Running was my thing. It was difficult at first due to my anxiety issues – and in particular anxiety attacks. Whenever on a run, my heart rate would elevate and my body assumed we were doing "that thing" again. I would never run far from my local park so when it happened, I got to a bench in the park as quickly as I could, lay on my back, and focused on counting my breaths. It confused Tungsten for a bit! The fact is, there is healing in sweating. It releases happy endorphins (ok, that bits not a fact. I've heard the science behind it, but I'm just better with laymen's terms and definitions). Due to my ex-tennis player battled body letting me down a bit (three torn calf muscles and a torn meniscus) I had to give up running. Hot yoga and pilates took over. I could walk into that hot room with the weight of the world on my shoulders. Upon leaving I had the same problems, they just didn't overwhelm me as much. I'll never forget the last hot yoga class I did. It was the first anniversary of Chris's death. I'd just celebrated our first wedding anniversary the day prior. I was not in a good headspace. Then the instructors asked us to get into a "dead body" pose. I had an anxiety attack in that room. A silent one. I didn't want to disturb the others. Yoga is a quiet, sacred practice. My instructor scolded me for not getting in the position. I stood up to leave but she told me I couldn't. I knew I couldn't leave the building – it's locked for security purposes. But I needed out of that room IMMEDIATELY. I never told her my personal story. But I did expect a yoga instructor to be all kumbaya and zen and realise people have life crap going on…and to just be kind. Anyway, adios. Never did that again. The point being, find the exercise you love to do. If you hate running, don't do it every day. God did not intend for you to spend one second of your life doing something you hate. Just find your thing and love it. Until you don't anymore, then find your next thing! And while I'm at it – nature. Get outside and breathe in the fresh air that we so often take for granted. Look at the sun and the bright blue sky. It's all pretty breathtaking. The satisfaction I get from walking my dog around the park is game-changing. I look up, let my face soak up the sun's rays, and take a moment to be intentionally and overwhelmingly grateful.

On the following page is a poem I recently penned about the first run I went on after returning from New York. My first attempt at exercise post-Bali. My first experience with anxiety. The only thing I want to mention here is that as awful as anxiety is, I've never died from it. I've always overcome it. It's horrific and real. A very difficult thing to understand if you haven't experienced it for yourself. Being a teacher, I've taught children that suffer from anxiety. I struggle as a mature adult to not let it win, what an incredibly difficult path to navigate for a child. It sneaks up on you and you are completely at its mercy. Plans must be changed, events cancelled and that is ok. I pray for anyone in the world today that in their day-to-day struggles with anxiety. I rarely suffer from it anymore; it doesn't have the stranglehold it did in my early stages of grief.

BREATHE

I look up
blue sky
sunshine
I smile
sweat trickling down my face
feet pounding the pavement
loud music in my headphones –
gone...the song ends.

There's a pause
A moment of quiet...
too
much
quiet.
My heart is beating out of my chest.

THUMP   THUMP   THUMP

My breath is short
no oxygen
Please...not now
I'm gasping for air
I beg my body to keep running,
to be normal,
to be unaffected
But it's out of my control
I'm drowning...
swallowed up WHOLE by the nothingness around me
Am I dying?

It has a name...
Anxiety.
Running was joyous.

But now, three weeks a widow.
And I can't breathe.
And nothing is as it was.
And never will it be again.

CHAPTER TWENTY SIX

"She made broken look beautiful and strong look invincible. She walked with the universe on her shoulders and made it look like a pair of wings."

– Ariana Dancu

Be Brave!

Being a school teacher I get twelve weeks of vacation leave a year. I'm so, so, so freaking blessed to get to travel. I promise I don't take it for granted. Taking some time out of "life" is imperative. Even a road trip to your favourite beach. I've returned to Lancelin too many times to count. I put on a good playlist, podcast, or I even spend some silent time with God. I pack a bag and just go! Let yourself breathe. It's needed. I don't travel so I can have cool Facebook posts (although they are!). I immerse myself in culture, meet new people, step out of my comfort zone and GROW from every single trip. My first solo trip was to Phuket, Thailand. I was thirty-one years old and I cried the entire day before leaving. See, in my head, I was saying final goodbyes. I left my will on the desk in my study. I said final goodbyes to my family members and my beloved Tungsten. As so often happened, intellectually I knew the chances of me dying on holiday were almost zero. But hey, so were Chris's. It's something I've had to work through. In my last two adventures, I had genuinely been excited for them and not cried. It's taken that long. Years of adventures – about 10 trips. Just imagine if I'd never boarded the plane in the first place because I let my fear consume me. I landed in Phuket and was internally a mess. You'd probably never know if you looked at me. On that trip, I ventured to the beach every single day for about six hours and spent the rest of the time in my hotel room, ordering room service, lacking the courage to do anything else. But, I mean, I was there right…talk about courage! Each day on the beach I poured over a book that I'm madly in love with to this day. "Dear Single Self" is written by the incredibly creative Amanda Viviers. Get a copy. Immediately. It helped me to rewire my thought process, not just behind my grief, but also my future. My copy of the book has notes written all through it and is highlighted and all sorts. Today I found this quote that I'd highlighted:

"Life is unpredictable,
It changes with the seasons,
Even your coldest winter,
Happens for the best of reasons,
And though it feels eternal,
Like all you'll ever do is freeze,
I promise spring is coming,
And with it, brand new leaves."
e.h.

Eighteen months after becoming a widow, these are the notes I scribbled under that quote.

My winter was my moment of greatest strength (with God). I could have checked out. But I didn't. I took it head-on. The hurt was great, deep, physical, and emotional. But penning this eighteen months later, the growth I see in myself is amazing. I love God. I love Chris. Because of them, I'm who I am today. And she is strong, compassionate, loving, full of life, generous, and humbled in gratitude.

Travel has taught me so much about myself and enabled growth. But it wasn't a passive thing. I had to venture out there and go get it. Since that December in 2015, I have travelled frequently solo and with friends or family. I've adventured to South Africa, the USA and Singapore a few times, Slovenia, Croatia, Thailand, Qatar, Portugal, Morocco, Hong Kong, Iceland, Italy, England, Paris, Peru, Argentina, Chile, Brazil, Uruguay, Ecuador, Ireland, Wales, France, and some domestic travel added for good measure. Each trip has required a huge step out of my comfort zone and the more I do it, the easier it's becoming. In October of 2017 I posted this to Facebook:

When Chris died, my life was a daily episode of doing things I didn't want to do. It was horrific. Burial vs cremation, when to fly home, how and when to tell people. Then it became bigger things - lawyer visits, psych visits, pastoral carer visits, and bank visits. Then it was heading back to work. Then it was the mundane daily stuff – name changes on accounts, mowing lawns, bins out, all the "his" jobs. There were so many firsts. At the time, they all made me sick. Every single one of them. Looking back now I realise doing all these things is what enabled the growth in me as a person.

I heard a quote a couple of years ago. "Everything you want is on the other side of fear." I heard this and booked a ten-day adventure through Morocco – beach, Sahara Desert, Marrakech city...because why not? Am I going to sit at home alone and be sad? No! Not when I only get one life to live. And you shouldn't either! Be brave! Jason Jaggard said it best in his book '*Spark*.' "Jesus doesn't invite you into a comfortable life. He invites us into a meaningful one...Apply for that job, date that person, move to that city, BUY THAT PLANE TICKET. Do all the things that scare you – because they're worth it." Man, that dude Jason has got it all sorted out. I mean, as I'm typing it I'm wondering, does he live this out? It's much easier to type than to live out, that is a fact. Also, a total expert on bravery is Brene Brown. Find her books or TED Talks. She's motivating, inspiring, and hilarious. Knowledge is power and I love reading, particularly with the end goal of personal growth. I'll finish this with one final thought that I found on the internet.

"Fill your life with adventure – not things! Have stories to tell, not stuff."

Amen to that.

CHAPTER TWENTY SEVEN

I pray that God, the source of hope, will fill you with joy and peace because you trust in Him. Then you will overflow with confident hope through the power of the Holy Spirit.

Romans 15:13 NIV

Hope

In my experience, God wants us to dream big and for our hearts to be overjoyed and bursting with hope for our futures. But in the last four years, I've learned that I can dream large, but what I think will be my future is ultimately out of my control. This isn't a reason to be fearful, it's a reason to relax, still, calm my anxieties, and know that it isn't in my control...because it's in God's. Who is more able and competent and loving and truly wants the best for me, more than Him?? Because of God and faith, we CAN have hope. In my situation, I believe it was too much for the human brain and human emotions to cope with. I can totally see the struggle that these huge life events can have on someone, I struggled and was at my absolute lowest, even with God. I believe that if it weren't for him and faith, instead of struggling to get out of bed after seven days, I maybe never would have. I would have walked around hollow, a vessel, no spark, no love, just a fragile shell existing and not living. After walking THROUGH those difficult days, and not shoving it down and pretending it doesn't exist, my spark was ignited again. I found joy, laughter, peace, happiness – all the good things that make life exceptional. I began to live a full life again. How can we have hope in a way that is both faith-filled and realistic? Here's my attitude about it. Someone recently asked me, "are you scared to be alone forever." I'd never been asked this. I took a moment to think about it. I don't usually think before I speak. But with honesty and thoughtfulness, I was able to answer. If I was asked that three years ago. It would have been a confident, scared, and anxious absolutely. The bible is filled with verses about marriage, the gifting of a partnership, and that life is better done with someone else. Add to that my desire to be a mother. Again, the bible speaks of the gifting of children. I'm a teacher, I have volunteered in the Kid's ministries at church, and being around children is my gifting from God. How could I not become a mother? I pray and dream for these things. But fast-forwarded to today...

fast-forwarded to today. I'm not scared of not fulfilling these dreams. If I were to not become a wife and mother, I'd be sad, and I'd have to grieve that my life path didn't include those things. But there are two reasons why it doesn't stress me out and make me anxious in my day to day. One – it's not in my control. I've given God complete control over my life. It doesn't mean I sit at home waiting on Him to produce miracles in my life (my guy isn't just going to knock on my front door). No. It's not meant to be a passive thing. I'm an active participant in my life. I go out, I online date, I date people that friends think I'd mesh with, I hang with amazing friends, I volunteer with amazing people, I'm doing Bible studies, I'm reading self-help books, I'm meeting with a psych, I'm traveling – I'm actively living my best life to give God every opportunity to allow my path to POTENTIALLY cross with my forever guy. The second thing that helps me remain calm is that my life is extraordinary. If I don't meet my guy, if I don't have children, if the way I live my life today is the way I'm destined to spend the next fifty years of my life, that is not a bad thing. In fact, it's an incredibly blessed and amazing life I get to adventure on each day. If I did continue this path, it may not be the path my heart had longed for, but if it's the path God has me on, it's perfect and as it should be. So when I dream, there is so much joy and privilege in dreaming big in line with God. I think as long as we centre our life on Him, let Him lead us, our life will be bigger and better than we can even imagine for ourselves. Honour your dreams by not being selfish and going your own way, honour them by leaning into God, listen to what he has to say, listen to what he places on your heart and follow that path.

This is some journaling from my Thailand trip.

> "It's in the quiet that God will invigorate my soul, allow me to better grow as a person as I patiently wait for Him to allow my life to unfold according to His plan."

I was a year into being a widow when I penned this. But it's so true. The only bit I'd change today is the word WAIT. I know the word patience intimately. God is often reminding me of it in our quiet time. But it's not something we sit around and do. Having hope is about "PASSIONATE waiting" as referred to in Lamentations. God is a God of miracles, but let's stack the odds in our favour, let's continue to grow and push our boundaries and LIVE every single day. Because they are precious. And I don't want to be the same as yesterday. I want to become a better person every single day that I have the privilege to wake up.

"Today I'm hopeful, grateful, thankful, encouraged. I'm determined to use this season in my life to become the BEST version of me. Let's do this!"

Further journaling from Thailand. It's not easy. Having hope when your heart is shattered (this isn't limited to the death of a loved one. It's finances, employment, relationships – life is TOUGH). I don't want you to think that Chris died and I woke the next day and participated in this journey of self-discovery and advancement free of the tough stuff. Nope. It all happened at the same time. The laughter, the tears, the anxiety, the hope, the anger, the love…it was and is an exhausting process. How do you think I got the age lines on my forehead?

God whispers promises into our hearts throughout the bible. Be faithful, open, and brave. Today is what it is. When God brings the spring and the new leaves, these are the promises of the life he wants you to have and you are the leaves, you can be restored and renewed. It's a team effort. Open your mind, your heart, and your eyes to the life God is preparing for you. In all seasons.

Finally, having hope is a choice. It's an active thing. You need to partner with God, listen to Him, listen to the directions he's sending you, where is He lighting the steps for you to take? Be faithful, be obedient and *choose* hope. Every single day. Not in a passive way either. It's an action. When you choose hope, life begins to sparkle again. Maybe not the life you had planned and dreamed for yourself. But the life God had planned for you. Don't sit around passively awaiting your dreams to tap you on the shoulder and come true. You will be waiting a while. And you will look back in two years, and you'll be the same you. Nothing wrong with that -I'm sure you're incredible. But God loves you too much to leave you as you are today. He has a plan for the incredible man or woman He wants you to be. Are you brave enough to step into the space? To dream big? To hope for the things on your heart that God wants for you? To step out of your comfort zone and attack this brilliant gift of life we've been given? To become these fierce, compassionate, faith-filled, loving humans God intended us to be all along? I pray you are.

CHAPTER TWENTY EIGHT

*"Saying nothing sometimes
says the most."*

- Emily Dickinson

Grief – How To, How Not To... How?

I remember vividly the looks I got from people the first time they saw me after Chris passed away. Whether it was a few days after I got home and an awkward glance in the supermarket. The smile as they see me, then the quick look away – oh crap, that's right, her husband died. Sometimes it was a month later being asked how my wedding was, then the uncomfortable facial expression and shock on their face. Or three years later when I'm asked why I wear my wedding rings on my right hand and the shock on the person's face as I recount my story. So here is the truth bomb. Honestly, your reaction, your words, your silence. It's ok. There isn't a procedure, protocol, or "How To" guide. It sucks. My best advice, if you don't know what to say, silence is the best. Don't ask how I am. I'm awful. And I was keeping it together until you asked. A simple squeeze of my shoulder as you walk past and a smile is all the encouragement needed. The grief is the absolute worst in the beginning weeks and months. Because as a human, you're lost, you're mechanical, you're a robot. You don't remember the kind gestures, the cards, the hugs at the funeral – actually, you don't even remember the funeral. Walking around zombie-like, but it's during this time you are surrounded constantly by people and asked non-stop how you are. It gets tricky after the first six months. People, society – opinions are formed and shared. Shouldn't you be over it now? You need to move forward, move on with your life. Opinions are normal, but keep it to yourself, please. Continue to show up and continue to be there, when everyone else has gone. Continue to speak of my person. I loved him and I still do. Speaking of him makes me smile, brings me joy, and doesn't hurt at all. Tell stories, laugh with me – it encourages my soul, brings me joy and I love it. If you're on my list of people I call crying hysterically, you're incredible and you're vital in my healing. Picking up your phone and listening to my tears, that was life-giving. LIFE. GIVING. In our western world, we are trained to put grief in a tidy little box and ignore it. We have no clue what to do. For tragedies of epic proportions, there's no rule book. Follow your heart quickly and use your mouth slowly. Also, a phrase I heard a lot in the initial grieving period – "it's what Chris would have wanted." Actually, you don't know that. Because he is not here. So decisions need to be based on today, not what you are guessing he would want. Because you don't know.

At team night at church recently we were given eight minutes of silence. Eight minutes. I get uncomfortable after two usually. I do love to fill a silence. It was about five minutes into that the silence and solitude that God spoke to me. "Continue to seek me, trust in me." I gave God a mental fist bump. You got it, man, we can do this. But next came a vision, the first time it had ever happened to me. God invited me to sit by still waters. There was a lake, and we were on the side on the greenest of grass. God had his legs crossed and I lay my head and upper body on his legs, he ran his hands through my hair. "My child, you've been lonely. Come to me in your loneliness."

It floored me. I didn't know I'd been lonely. He knows me better than I know me. Why was I so shocked, of course, he does…but he'd never revealed it (or I'd never given him space to reveal it if we're going to be honest) to me in such a blatant way before. I'm so busy on my path to heal and grow that I lost sight of my heart. It was time to change that. It was also a huge reminder, that when no one understands what we are going through or we feel isolated, God gets it. God gets us, more than we get ourselves! God is with us.

Apparently, several people felt that I was running away by heading to New York. As humans, we make judgements, because often we can't help it. But here are some little truths about grief. Firstly, grief should be one hundred percent free of judgment. There are no road maps, and it's different for everyone. So what a person chooses to do is absolutely what should be done. You can have your opinions on it, but just keep them to yourself. Secondly, grief isn't isolated to occurring only in one space. My grief, and in turn, healing, in those initial three weeks, took place in Indonesia, Australia, and America. But factually – it was taking place in my heart and my head. Regardless of where I was globally, or which house I was in, which town I was in, my grief was within me, as was my healing. So to everyone reading this – you do you. Grieve how you want to and how you think you should. Go for it. As the saying goes, haters gonna hate. And you know what, the haters are often in fact lovers. They are the people that love you the most and want nothing but the best for you and they offer their advice because, in their mind, that's how they can help you. Because they love you and they are grieving for you. For your loss. For your divorce, unemployment, finances, health, relationships – whatever it may be. In this day and age, there is so much to grieve for. I'm permitting you to do it the way you want. But of course – you don't even need my permission.

My final advice – don't put a wedding card and sympathy card in the same envelope. Two envelopes...every...single...time.

CHAPTER TWENTY NINE

At some point, you just have to let go of what you thought should happen and live in what is happening."

- Heather Hepler

Life Wasn't Meant To Be Easy

It just wasn't. I think that sucks. When I look back at the depths of my sadness and heartache, I would pray no one else had to ever experience that. But I feel like that would be said in a whimsical, child-like ignorance that we all know just isn't true. I remember having a great chat with a dear friend that is a Disney princess (I know – epic!!!) about Disney films and how they paint life as a fairytale and all the dreams come true for the princesses. Her reply shifted my perspective. She believed these princesses often had to overcome horrendous hardship before they got to the happy ending. I've compared my story to a Nicholas Sparks romance novel, perhaps I make myself a Zebra, the main character, and we have the next great Disney story?? My beautiful friend Monja created the picture below based on a diagram I found online. A picture does speak a thousand words.

I think a lot of Christians believe that being Christian gives them a cloak of invisibility preventing them from any hardships life might have to offer. But it's not the case. Stay steadfast, even when you're at your lowest and feel heartbroken and defeated. Our God is the God of miracles. He will champion for you – but you must let Him. On the next page is a poem I wrote when I reminisced over those early days and the hardships I faced and the feeling of despair and desperation. Fast forward three years and with a new lens, new perspective, you can look back and realise that your journey is a rebuilding process. One that is remarkable and worthy of celebration.

REBUILT

My heart bleeds
It's heavy
Burdened
Saddened
Broken
No... shattered.

What was once filled with love, life, laughter, joy
Is no more.
But not forever
In time...
When?
Slowly
Slowly
Slowly
Step by step
Hour by hour
Day by day
The love, life, laughter, joy
Creeps back in
Like wax under a hot iron
It spreads to every crevice
Of my life-giving heart

And it's not the same
And it never will be
And it's OK

Because my heart was rebuilt
A new version of itself
An upgrade
Stronger, wiser, humbled, loved, grateful
Forever changed.
To look like God always intended it to.

CHAPTER THIRTY

"*I think we dream so we don't have to be apart for so long. If we're in each other's dreams, we can be together all the time.*"

- A.A. Milne

I'll See You In My Dreams

It was months until I had a dream about Chris. I spent far too long analysing what that meant. Why did it have to mean anything? I hear stories of people that have these realistic, fluffy dreams of their loved ones and I'm in the corner thinking, I sleep hard for eight hours a night. I've had nada. About a week before my first dream of Chris, I was back at work and was almost done with all the lawyer and bank appointments and my new normal was formed. It was around this time I was told of all the rumours going around about everything that happened. That I was pregnant, that I had died, that Chris had been decapitated… it was horrific. I cried myself silly all through the night. Some things we don't need to hear. But it can't be unheard. This all weighed so heavily on my heart and I think perhaps that brought on the dream. In my dream, I was in our bedroom with Chris, and I was brushing the curls of a little girl. They were my horrific curls, so I knew she must have been my daughter. When I was done brushing her hair, she went to a small cot by our bed. Then Chris and I got into bed and held hands as we fell asleep. Quick, short, and nothing earth-shattering. I woke up the next morning, and my hands were clasped together. An odd way to sleep really. It took a minute to realise I wasn't holding Chris's hand, I was holding my own. I had woken up and forgotten that he'd died. When I pulled my own clasped hands out from under the bed cover I was hysterical. Chris had died. It's like I'd been told all over again. It was a struggle to get to school that day. I think God sent me that dream. Just a quick, peaceful, heart-hugging moment in time (even if it was in my sleep) to bring me comfort. That was it. I haven't had one since. And that's ok too. I know he's in heaven watching down, making sure I'm doing him proud. I think I don't dream of him because God's got him. What more could my heart want than for that?

CHAPTER THIRTY ONE

*"When you are going through
something hard and wonder
where God is, remember the
teacher is always quietest
during a test"*

– Anonymous

Test Of Faith

I went on the most spectacular six-week tour of South America in December/ January of 2018/19. It was on this trip I decided that as soon as I got back to Perth I'd book an appointment to see a specialist about my fertility. The narrative is so common with this. I was thirty four, over the hill, single. Society told me I must panic and make a plan. In my heart, I felt at peace about all of that, because I knew God's life plan for me was to be a mother. But before this trip, it hit home that there was a family history of fertility difficulties and I learned that my Mum started menopause at fourty two. Both not great signs for me as far as my journey goes. My fears were confirmed and I found out I had geriatric eggs. They were old. Well, they probably weren't, but the quantity of them was that of an older person. This tested my faith. Was it not enough to be a widow in one lifetime? I now had to go through this journey? As with every speed bump in life, I took time to be sad, then to be angry, and then I made a plan because I was living in 2019 and God created some brilliant minds that give women like me options. So I began my first round of egg freezing. Basically the same process as IVF, but stopping before the egg gets fertilised. Again, it was sitting in waiting rooms alone, ticking the widow box. Then there were injections, feeling off mentally and physically because of the hormones... and doing it all by myself. I know it's a blessing being able to do IVF, and when I'm well mentally, I see that so clearly. But when I'm not, it's difficult to see past the dark cloud of doubt and insecurity. That first round saw my surgeon retrieve 9 eggs, 6 of which were viable for freezing. In 2020, when Covid-19 calmed down in Western Australia and elective surgeries were again taking place, I completed my second round. This was so much more intense than the first, perhaps because the dosage of my injections was increased in the hope they'd retrieve more eggs. I felt every injection so much more, I burst so many blood vessels in my stomach with my injections that I looked like I'd gone eight rounds with Mike Tyson, I cried…a lot, and I held a two-week-long pity party for myself. Although I'm not proud of it, I recognise my body didn't feel like my own for 5 weeks. To add to all of that, 6 eggs were retrieved, and only 5 were viable for freezing. I was uncomfortable the entire time during my injections and I had small amounts of bleeding days after my surgery, before beginning my period 7 days early. Do you know what I did? I began my period and called my specialist to book my next round. I needed one more round. So I was just going to do it. Two rounds down and one to go. Currently, eleven eggs are sitting in a freezer labelled with my name. I have a low egg count and am just so grateful that in this day and age, I have options. It's incredibly tough, physically and mentally, but it's worth it if it means realising my dream of being a Mum. I posted this to Facebook before I began my second round. Because people don't talk about it, and they absolutely should. It's also nothing to be ashamed of, and so many women are going through it.

POSTED TO FACEBOOK September 2020:

Well…first blood test today and injections start tomorrow…for my second round of IVF for egg freezing. Yup, I have the gift of a glitch in the fertility area. Through no fault of my own, like becoming a widow, I've been dealt the path less desired. What I've come to realise is, I'm not that special. Women every single day are learning they struggle with fertility, yet it's rarely talked about. So here I am starting a conversation. I'm so grateful this is happening to me in 2020 when there are more options available. But still, even with IVF, women are struggling to conceive and it's devastating.

It's my prayer that one day when I'm ready, I'll be able to have children of my own. But until that day, I'm doing all I can to stack the odds in God's favour. So, here's to the next fourteen days of self-injecting, blood tests, scans, bloating, nausea, and hopefully/prayerfully … more than the eggs that were retrieved in round one.

P.S. Super stoked to journey with some amazing family and friends – love you all!

#bythegraceofgod #thankyoumedicare #girlpower

"My grace is all you need. My power works best in the weakness." – 2 Corinthians 12:9 NIV

"Don't be afraid. Just believe." – Mark 5:36 NIV

"One day it just clicks, you realise what's important and what isn't. You learn to care less about what other people think of you and more about what you think of yourself. You realise how far you've come and you remember when things were such a mess that you would never recover. And you smile. You smile because you are truly proud of yourself and the person you've fought to become."
-Unknown

Happily Ever After...

Written in October 2019:

Did I write this story too soon? Before my happily ever after? Well, here's what I think. I think every day is my happily ever after. If I compile a list of what my heart desires out of life, a husband and children would be the only two things on it. But if I compiled a list of what delights my heart that I already have...let's just say I'd need fifty more chapters in this book. Because my life is incredibly blessed. I continue to hope in God for a future that has a husband and children, but I'm now so reliant on Him and firmly trust that He is in control of my future. If my life doesn't head in that direction, it will be because He has something even more incredible planned for me. Coming to that conclusion almost four years after losing Chris has released so much anxiety and worry from my life. Grateful is my mantra and grateful to God I will forever be. I'm obsessed with all aspects of my life – the people in it, how I spend each day, who I am, my journey so far – ALL OF IT. Yes, even losing Chris.

Honestly, that day in Bali was the worst thing that happened to me. That day my husband went to heaven. But, nothing else bad came from it. Only good. I have a whole new perspective on life. I get ridiculous amounts of joy from a sunset, blue skies, being in a park, coffee with the ones I love – things that I took for granted before. I didn't have to lose Chris to learn these lessons, but God doesn't let these hardships in life be in vain. He can work good from it. I love who I was before that day, but the woman I am now is someone I'm immensely proud of. Because it was all due to decisions I made. Deciding to show up and not give up, every single day. No matter how much I wanted to.

To sum it up I'll tell you this. The people in my world are the best. My job as a first-grade teacher, although challenging, brings me ridiculous joy and purpose every single second I spend at it. I travel as often as my finances allow. I live in a home I love with the best roommate a gal could ask for – my dog Tungsten. I volunteer at my church I feel at home in, brokenness and all. I have sponsor kids and as often as I can I give to the various organisations around my city and the world to help give voices to the most vulnerable people in it because my heart insists I do. In my own little way, I'm trying to make the world a slighter better place than when I came into it. It's the least I can do for a God that has walked my path of grief so lovingly with me. When I think about it too much, I get overwhelmed by how good God has been to me. I feel so undeserving. But that's the kind of God I serve. Loyal and on team Tara, wanting nothing more than all my dreams to come true.

After reading the words on these pages, woven together from my heart to paper, I am compelled even more to live like a hummingbird. The desire to experience love, joy and have celebration radiating from within my heart is overwhelming. I pray you feel it too, the longing to live the most spectacularly rich life and enjoy all that it has to offer. Because that is exactly what it is supposed to be, spectacular. If God was able to take my mundane, yet happy life through the depths of a dark grave and grow the most beautifully vibrant garden, He can absolutely do it for you too.

I wrote this chapter just shy of four years into my journey as a widow. I had this manuscript all wrapped up in a neat little bow and sent off to my editor. I wrote about continuing to live out of my comfort zone, questioning whether I wrote this story too soon, before my happily ever after. Then recognising that if I live the rest of my life how I spend my days today, I would be incredibly blessed. The recognition that although the bible speaks of life done in unity between a husband and wife, it doesn't lessen the value of life done in the company of great friends and family. And then, it happened...

CHAPTER THIRTY THREE

And one day
you will look back
and see that all along,
the HOPE that you chose
to audaciously believe in long ago,
has always been real,
making space for you to grow,
making room for you to heal.
For even when the waves
washed you into the boat
and knocked you to your knees
hope was still the anchor.
You did not sink.
You did not fail.

- MHN

Epilogue

Written in September 2021:

As it happened, in God's timing and through the courage of attending many coffee dates through online dating, I met my person. And he is so different from Chris. Which is great. Not in a good nor a bad way. In a way that states he isn't Chris and he is an incredible human being in his own right. On November 2nd 2019, after attending a friend's wedding and fixing a flat battery, I made it, albeit late, to the greatest first date with a bright blue-eyed man (God knows how to pick them for me) with a beautiful smile who made me laugh through coffee, which turned to dinner. I was smitten. On our first date after that, he had planned a ferry ride into the city, dinner at a vegetarian restaurant, and dessert back in South Perth. It was thoughtful and my heart was pleased. It was that night that I prayed to God and told him "You know I'm a terrible judge of character. If this is my guy, just make it obvious. Like super obvious." And of course, in reply, I got stone-cold silence. Nada. Nothing. Gah! A few days later the words 'birthday' and 'birthdate' were placed on my heart - for quite a few days. It was very confusing and something you would just miss if it weren't for what happened one evening at dinner. He asked me my birthdate. After telling him mine, I asked for his. He said "March 9th," to which I said "1979?" I got immediate goose bumps. It was Chris's exact birthdate. God let me know that this was my guy and he was my future. He looked over at me concerned, but I waited till later that evening and over text message explained what God had placed on my heart. I would learn later that four years before we met, he also had a word from God. He was told he would meet a woman who had lost her husband. It gives me chills. To think that four years ago amid my grief and darkest hours, God was orchestrating a beautiful future.

Taylor Swift wrote a song called "Invisible String" and the lyrics are beautiful, reminding me that God perhaps had us tied together long before we met. Here is a snippet.

> *"Time, mystical time cuttin' me open then healin' me fine. Were there clues I didn't see? And isn't it just so pretty to think, all along there was some invisible string tying you to me."*

The past couple of years have been filled with so much joy, laughter and love. God prepared him for the unique situation of dating a widow. He took up a huge space in my heart very early on. Then there is little Tungsten. Those two boys are as thick as thieves. It's like he's forgotten the last eight years we've spent together – out with the old, in with the new. But honestly, it warms my heart. We are two years into our journey together and we have already navigated mountain tops and valleys like we are promised in the bible, but there isn't anyone else I'd rather be adventuring through them with. I'm filled with hope for my future because God is continuing to lead me.

My heart is full and my life is breathtaking.

> *"God is not in the business of leaving*
> *things broken and messy.*
> *He's not a God that sees a hard*
> *situation and shrugs, and says,*
> *"I guess I'm not really*
> *sure what to do with this one."*
> *He's a God that brings life from death,*
> *beauty from ashes, hope from despair,*
> *light from darkness, and healing from*
> *the most broken,*
> *mixed up, and messy situations."*
> *-Stephanie May Wilson*

Prayers

Pastoral carer extraordinaire Nicki Bowles wrote these prayers for me. If you have never prayed, here's a starting point for you. If you have, but you have lost your way, find it again. Finally, if you pray daily – awesome, keep at it!

Prayer for those who are new to talking to God:

Dear God,

I don't know you that well, but today I want to say that I believe that you are present in this world even if I can't see you, and that you are listening to my prayer. Thank you for creating this world, and for creating me. The bible tells us that you are love, and so I receive your love today. I thank you that you never leave me alone and that you have a plan for my life that I can live out if I live it with you. I will hold onto you in the hard times and rejoice with you in the good times.

Please show me the way.

Amen

For those who do talk to God:

Dear God,

Thanks for hearing my prayers and for being with me in the hard times and the good times. Thank you, Jesus, for walking by my side. I believe that life is best lived your way, so I want to take your hand and follow you along the path that you have prepared for me. Thanks for never leaving me and never giving up on me. I receive your love today.

Amen

Notes

Throughout my grief journey in which I adventured into the land of self-improvement, books were a really integral part of my experience. I would furiously jot down notes in the columns, highlight quotes that resonated, place ear folds on important pages, post it notes placed throughout...I was addicted. Below are all the amazing books and a podcast that are part of my collection, helping me along the way! Thank you to every single creative soul - you spoke to my heart.

Jason Jaggard:
Spark: Transform Your World, One
Small Risk at a Time

Brene Brown:
Braving The Wilderness
Daring Greatly

Amanda Viviers:
Dear Single Self
Dear Creative Self
Embracing Slow and Pause: New
Year Vision Day Book
www.amandaviviers.com

Jodie McCarthy:
Beauty in the Ashes
Grace & Space
www.jodiemccarthy.com

Hank Fortener:
Podcast – Hank Presents

William P. Young:
The Shack

Ann Voskamp:
One Thousand Gifts

Acknowledgements

Chris – Squishy…Our time, although short, is forever stored in my heart. I learned so much through our time together, and through losing you. Thank you for choosing me. For a person that loves words, there just aren't any. But you know exactly how my heart feels and I look forward to seeing you again in heaven one day. I love you…

Noel – My biggest supporter- a weirdo like me, a heart the size of Texas, the master of all Dad jokes, my adventure buddy and my person. The sun shines brighter having you in my heart. You turned my grey world into a kaleidoscope of bright colours. Here's to many more years of laughter and adventure. I love you.

Tungsten – You can't read…but that doesn't matter. You're my best friend and have loved me unconditionally since the day we got you. You walked this journey with me (sometimes abandoning me – but that's ok). I love you little guy.

Family – In Australia and South Africa. The saying "I got you," it's not a saying to me. You all actively actioned it. You were there. My world stopped, I couldn't breathe and you were there. That's true love. I fear I don't have the words to truly convey my love and gratitude for every single one of you. We've navigated difficulty, time and time again. But we've laughed hard. So hard. We have beautiful memories, and we have a future to fill with more. You have my unconditional love and support always. The Brownings and the Claassens – two families that represent love, dependency, trust, happiness, and strength. It is a privilege to know you all. If you weren't my family, I'd choose you as my friends. I love you.

To my Mum and Dad – this sentence has sat here empty for an incredibly long time. That's because the support and love you two have given me from the day I was born is astronomical. I am the person I am because of you two. I'm so grateful that I had such an awesome childhood and grew up believing I could do and be anything. You both continue to support me every day, in the big things and the mundane, and we are still laughing every step of the way. Thank you isn't enough. My journey would have looked completely different if I didn't have you two on my team. *Jason and Caris* – middle born child is always the best. It's in print. It must be true. Glad we're related, but I'd hang with ya'll regardless. *Chris, Annelie, JC, Charlene, Jandre and Netta* – family by marriage, but friends absolutely by choice. Meeting Chris all those years ago, I could never have imagined the quality of people that would be added to my world. In your grief at losing your son and brother, you remained steadfast in your love and support for me. Always and forever grateful. Love you guys.

Friends – To name you would be a long task and I fear I'd forget someone. You know who you are. You've journeyed with me and you've been steadfast. Through the ups and downs and I know I've tested your patience, and yet, I awake and you're still here. My tribe, my team – thank you. From the depths of my heart and soul, my life is spectacular in large to you who are in it. Near, far, those I speak to daily and those I speak to yearly. You are special and I love you.

Roschel – Thanks for picking up the phone every single time (except that one night!). You agreed with me when I cried and said the situation sucked, you told me when I needed to put on my big girl knickers and you were there every day since the hospital. You and your family are truly the greatest humans.

JP – Your perspective on life and your encouragement to live mine to the fullest is everything and I cherish you.

Michelle – Forever grateful to you for all you did over that period. So proud to call you my bestie!

Nicki Bowles, pastoral carer extraordinaire and friend – Thank you for listening through my tears and laughing at my jokes (even the bad ones). Blessed am I.

The Team – Em, the greatest editor, thank you for giving me the confidence to make this story the best it could be. Kellie – thank you for providing the creative spark I often lack! Amanda and Jodie – thanks for taking time, making space and endless encouragement. Monja – your creativity rocks. Appreciate your help and your friendship every single day!

Riverview Church – the pastors, the guest preachers, the team, the volunteers, the people – THE HEARTBEAT. Through my journey, you have spoken the Word so poetically, truthfully and in a way that resonated in my heart. You helped me breathe when I couldn't by myself. You navigated the storm with me, and the beauty of that is you probably don't even know it.

Huntingdale Primary – How blessed was I that my world crashed when I was surrounded and held up by such quality humans as ya'll. We don't see each other often. And some of you I may never see again. You all played a profoundly important role in my grieving in that first year. Thank you from the bottom of my heart. I never took a single one of you for granted, nor will I ever.

Victoria Park Primary – Stepping in at the half time interval, you effortlessly helped me navigate my path into true healing and were part of my new beginning. Such great people. Blessed by ya'll daily.

To you reading this – I'm so thankful to you. Thank you for being an active part of my journey. I pray you read these pages and are filled with hope and inspiration to be the best you. Life was meant to be lived incredibly day by day. I pray you do, wildly and unabashedly. Live. For those we love that no longer have the privilege.

God – Those waves crashed and pulled me under, and you were faithful...you left the 99. It's all for you, and it's all because of you. It begins and ends...with you. You are the light...it's not a passage of scripture. It is as real to me as the sun rising every morning. I know I fall short every single day, but thank you for your grace, forgiveness and for loving me.

9780645293111